SIMONE GOODING

LITTLE *traveller*

10 small felt intrepid explorers and 30 tiny travel accessories to sew

TUVA

Tuva Publishing
www.tuvapublishing.com

Address Merkez Mah. Cavusbasi Cad. No:71
Cekmekoy - Istanbul 34782 / Turkey
Tel: +9 0216 642 62 62

Little Traveller

First Print 2018 / February

All Global Copyrights Belong To
Tuva Tekstil ve Yayıncılık Ltd.

Content Sewing

Editor in Chief Ayhan DEMİRPEHLİVAN
Project Editor Kader DEMİRPEHLİVAN
Designer Simone GOODING
Technical Editors Leyla ARAS, Büşra ESER
Graphic Designers Simone GOODING, Ömer ALP,
Abdullah BAYRAKÇI, Tarık TOKGÖZ
Photograph and Illustrations Simone GOODING

ISBN 978-605-9192-36-1

f TuvaYayincilik ⓟ TuvaPublishing
t TuvaYayincilik ⓘ TuvaPublishing

Contents

Projects

A world of Whimsy and Adventure

Step inside the enchanting world of characters created by artist Simone Gooding.

Containing a mixture of charming illustrations and photographs to help bring these beautiful animals and dolls to life. In this craft book you will find a variety of whimsical animals and dolls with their accessories to stitch, knit and make.

Travel along with these little folk as they gather all they need to explore the small world that surrounds them.

You will find a tiny girl and her large bear companion, a squirrel gathering acorns in her knitted basket staying warm in her felt cape, a small hedgehog ready for the snow in his splendid felt sleigh and many more.

With 10 original 100% wool felt animals and dolls to make, along with 30 cosy knitwear, snuggly felt or soft linen accessories 'Little Traveller" provides all the inspiration and know-how needed to bring each character to life.

Simone Gooding

page 70

page 50

Mail

.... xx

page 38

page 28

materials & notions

100% wool hand dyed felt

I have been using this wonderful fabric for many years now. It is very strong but also wonderfully soft so performs beautifully every time. I highly recommend you use very high quality wool felt, poor quality or synthetic felt will not withstand the small seam allowance, tight turning of pieces and firm stuffing required. I use Winterwood felt.

buttons

For many years now I have been collecting vintage buttons. I just love to use vintage buttons, they have such wonderful colours, patterns and designs. My favourites are made of Bakelite Plastic from the 1950's and 60's. I have used a few of them thoughout the projects in this book.

yarn

I just love knitting and always use very high quality natural yarn. I recently discovered a gorgeous Sheltland yarn from the Shetland Isles. The soft heathered texture gives a lovely finish. I have used Jamieson's Naturally Spindrift Double Knitting yarn thoughout this book. It is 4ply and is perfect for small knitted garments.

vilene heavy backing

Vilene Heavy Backing is a strong, 'iron on' fabric that is very thick and is used to thicken felt and other fabrics. I have used it in the sleigh, mailbox, boat and tent.(see instructions) it is available at most fabric and craft supply shops.

knitted stitch guide & abbreviations

increasing

Increase, by working twice into the same stitch. Work in this way when asked to 'increase'

make one

Make one stitch. This method of increasing is worked in the horizontal strand of yarn that lies between the stitch you have just knited (0n the right hand needle) and the next stitch on the left hand needle. First, pick up the horizontal strand of yarn with the point of the left hand needle knitwise, that is from front of work to the back of work. Next, knit into the back of it, thus forming a new stitch. Work in this way when you see 'm1'

french knot instructions and diagrams

Pull the needle up from the back of the fabric to the front.
Place the needle in front of the floss

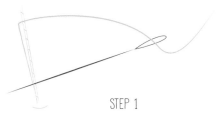

STEP 1

Wind the floss around the needle twice.
Continue the tension of the floss with your left hand (non-needle hand) to prevent it from uncoiling.

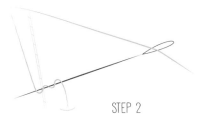

STEP 2

Keeping the coil of thread nice and tight around the needle, re-insert the tip of your needle just next to, but not into the same exit point on your fabric.

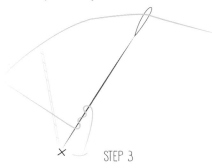

STEP 3

Pull the thread slowly and firmly until you have a tight small knot.

STEP 4

daisy stitch instructions and diagrams

Bring the thread up from the back of the fabric and re-insert the needle back in to the same hole.

STEP 1   A

Bring the needle back up through the fabric at a spot just next to where you started.
Making sure you push it through the loop in the thread

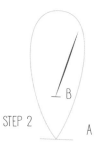

STEP 2   B   A

Push the needle back down through a third hole. Making sure the thread is over the end of the loop.

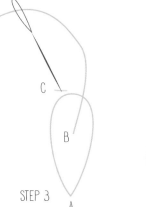

C   B

STEP 3   A

setting the eye

1 Mark the position of the eyes with pins.

2 Cut a long piece of upholstery thread and thread it through the metal loop at the back of the eye.

3 Thread a long doll making needle with both ends of the thread, and push the needle through the front of the face at the position of the first pin.

Bring the needle out in the stuffing at the neck.

4 Take the needle off the thread and thread the needle again with only one length of the thread.

Push the needle up through the stuffing and out of the face right next to one side of the eye. Repeat with the remaining thread on the other side of the eye.

5 Take the two lengths of thread that are poking out on either side of the eye and tie a triple knot, pulling it tight so the knot is hidden behind the back of the eye.

6 Now thread the needle again with one of the lengths of thread and push the needle back in next to the eye and out through the stuffing in the neck.

Repeat with the remaining thread.

7 Tie a triple knot in the stuffing in the neck a few times until the eye is secure. Repeat steps 1-7 again with the remaining eye.

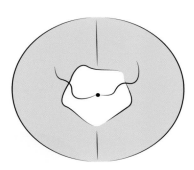

head gusset diagram

Make in this way for : Mr Oak, Thistle, Bear and Twig

a   b   c

finished back of head

body gusset diagram

Make in this way for : Mr Oak, Thistle and Fig Newton

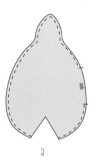 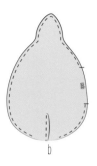 

a   b   c

finished body

stitching doll head and hair diagram

Make in this way for all dolls.

stitching arm diagram

Make in this way for all dolls and animals except Snail.

a   b

stitching leg / feet diagram

Make in this way for: Purslane, Thistle, Mr Oak and Fig Newton

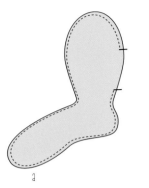 

a   b

attaching arms diagram

Work in this way for all dolls and animals except Snail.

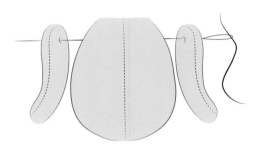

attaching legs diagram

Work in this way for : Mr Oak, Fig Newton and Thistle

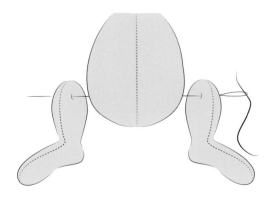

projects

Little Sisters...

What a beautiful new tent! what lucky little girls you are Daisy and Betty

daisy & betty
go camping

Daisy and Betty measure: 13cm (5") tall - Tent measures: 18cm x 18cm (7"x 7")

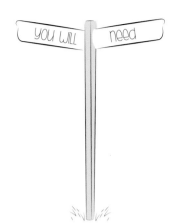

DAISY AND BETTY GO CAMPING

TEMPLATES ON PAGES 104-106

DOLLS

 30cm x 13cm (12"x 5") peach wool felt for both dolls' head and arms

🍎 18cm x 10cm (7"x 4") aqua wool felt for Daisy's body top and sleeves

🍎 20cm x 7cm (8"x 3") white wool felt for Daisy's body bottom pieces

🍎 18cm x 9cm (7"x 3½") lemon wool felt for Daisy's hood

🍎 10cm x 5cm (4"x 2") caramel wool felt for Daisy's hair and plaits

🍎 15cm (6") long piece of thin ribbon for Daisy's plaits

🍎 20cm x 13cm (8"x 5") lemon wool felt for Betty's body

🍎 18cm x 13cm (7"x 5") red wool felt for Betty's hood and collar

🍎 12cm x 8cm (5"x 3") black wool felt for Betty's head and hair

🍎 7cm (3") long piece of ribbon for Betty's bow

🍎 x2 4mm English glass dolls eyes for each doll

🍎 Gutermann Upholstery thread for attaching the eyes

🍎 Long doll making needle

🍎 Sewing machine thread to match the felt

🍎 Black embroidery thread

🍎 x1 vintage /novelty button for each doll

🍎 Toy fill

🍎 General sewing supplies

SLEEPING POUCHES

🍎 24cm x 16cm (9½"x 6½") wool felt for each sleeping pouch

🍎 24cm x 16cm (9½"x 6½") fabric for each sleeping pouch

🍎 x1 vintage /novelty button for each sleeping pouch

PILLOWS

🍎 10cm x 8cm (4"x 3") fabric for each pillow

🍎 Contrasting embroidery thread

🍎 Toy fill

TENT

🍎 71cm x 63cm (28" x 25") wool felt for the tent

🍎 38cm x 36cm (15"x 14") Vilene Heavy Backing for tent

🍎 13cm x 8cm (5"x 3") leaf green wool felt for leaves

🍎 8cm x 8cm (3"x 3") lemon wool felt for flowers

🍎 80cm (31½") long piece of ribbon for tent

🍎 24cm (9½") long piece of thin black elastic for tent

🍎 x4 toggle buttons for tent

🍎 Sewing machine thread to match felt

A very tiny seam allowance is needed and included for Daisy, Betty, the sleeping pouches and the tent, 3mm on all pieces

A scant 1/4" seam allowance is used for the pillow

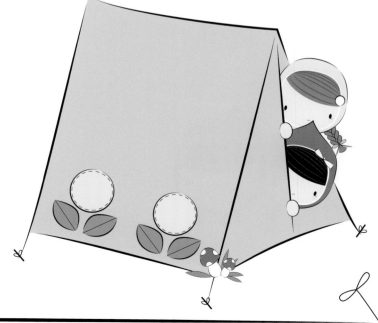

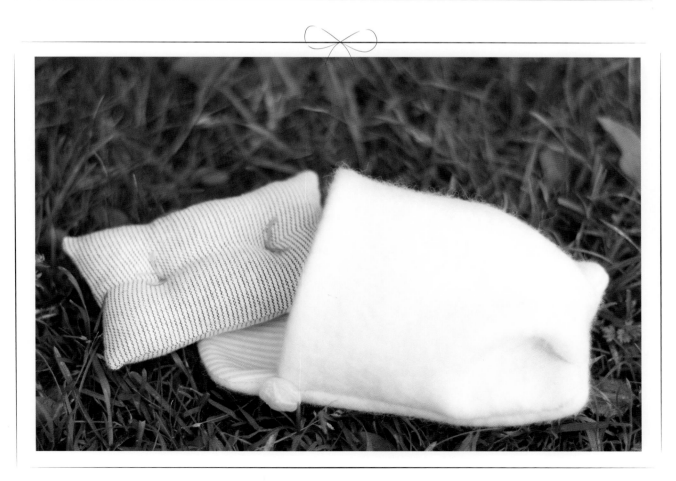

DAISY'S HEAD

* Stitching Doll Head and Hair Diagrams are on page 12

1 Place the hair piece on top of the peach head piece as marked. Using matching thread to the hair on your sewing machine, top stitch across the hair.

2 With right sides together, stitch around the outer edge of the head, leaving open at the bottom where indicated.

3 Turn the head right side out and stuff very firmly. The head circumference should measure approx. 16½cm (6½")

4 Mark the position for the eyes with pins. Attach the English glass eyes per instructions on page 11 using Gutermann Upholstery Thread to match the felt. Anchor your thread inside the stuffing in the head opening.

5 Using two strands of black embroidery thread, stitch a small back stitch in place as the mouth.

DAISY'S BODY

1 Cut two body top pieces from aqua felt and two body bottom pieces from white felt. Match the straight edge of the top piece to one long straight edge of the bottom piece and stitch. Repeat with the remaining body top and bottom piece.

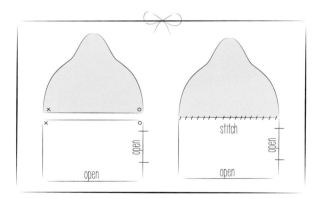

2 With right sides together, machine stitch all the way around the body, leaving open where indicated at the side and bottom.

3 Machine stitch the base oval in place, turn the body right side out and stuff firmly. Stitch the opening in the side closed.

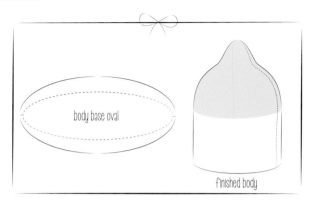

body base oval

finished body

4 Make a small indent with your finger in the opening in the head and push the neck of the body inside the head, hold the head on with pins while you stitch the head in place, tucking under the raw edge of the felt as you go.

stitch

DAISY'S ARMS

1 Stitch the arms all the way around, leaving open where indicated, turn right side out and place a small amount of stuffing in to the 'hands', close the openings on the arms. Leave aside for now.

SLEEVES

1 Cut four sleeves from aqua felt and stitch two of them all the way around, leaving open at the straight edge. Repeat with the remaining two sleeves.

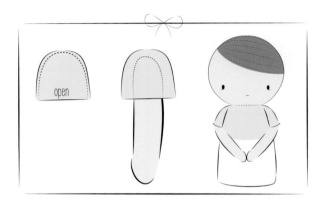

2 Slide an arm inside each sleeve, pin the arms to each side of the body just under the head. With two strands of Gutermann Upholstery Thread and a long doll making needle, stitch right through one arm and sleeve through the body and out the other side of the other arm, keep going through in this fashion many times until the arms are firm, fasten off.
(see Attaching Arms Diagram on page 12)

3 Place a few tiny stitches in the 'hands' to hold them at the front.

DAISY'S HOOD

1 Cut one hood front and one hood back from lemon felt. Place them together and stitch all the way around the outer curved edge, leaving open where indicated.

2 Turn the hood right side out and slide it on to the head. Add a few stitches at the back to hold it in place.

3 Stitch a small vintage/novelty button to her hair.

DAISY'S PLAITS

1 For the plaits, cut six pieces of felt to match the hair that measure - 2" x ½" (5cm x 1½"cm).

2 Place three tiny pieces on top of each other and add a small stitch in one end just to hold them together.

3 Plait the three sections of felt and tie the end in a bow with a piece of thin ribbon.

4 Repeat with the remaining tiny pieces of felt.

5 Stitch the end of one plait to the side of the front of the head just under the hood. Repeat with the remaining plait on the other side of the head.

BETTY

* Make Betty's head and hair in the same way as Daisy. To make her body and arms follow the Evie pattern on page 32.

BETTY'S HOOD

1 Cut one hood front and one hood back from red felt. Place them together and stitch all the way around the outer curved edge, leaving open where indicated.

2 Turn the hood right side out, making sure to push right in to the point. Add a little stuffing to the top, pointy tip and slide it on to the head. Hand stitch the open side edges closed, making sure to tuck in a tiny raw edge as you stitch.

3 Make a tiny bow from a short length of ribbon and stitch to the front of the hood.

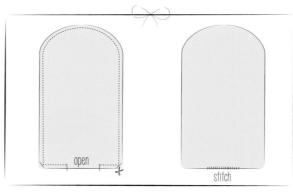

4 Cut one collar from red felt. Gather along the top curved edge of the collar. Wrap it around the neck, pull the gathers to fit and add a few stitches to hold it at the front. Stitch a small vintage/novelty button to the front of the collar.

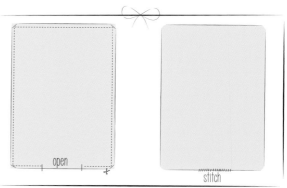

3 Create a pleat in the centre of one of the long sides of the sleeping pouch cover approx. 1″ long. Add a few stitches to hold it in place.

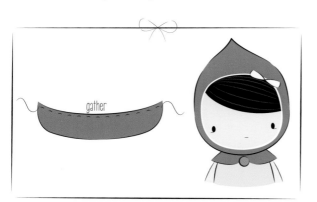

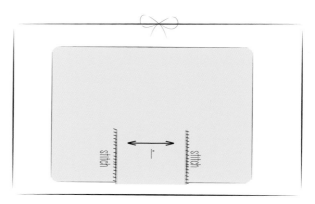

SLEEPING POUCH

1 Cut one fabric and one felt sleeping pouch base piece. With right sides together, stitch all the way around, leaving open where indicated. Clip the corners, turn right side out and press. Hand stitch the opening closed.

2 Repeat with the sleeping pouch cover piece.

4 With fabric sides facing. Hand stitch the cover to the base as shown below.

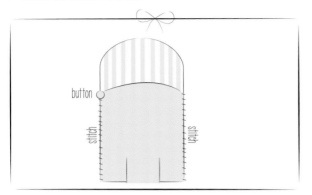

5 Stitch a vintage/novelty button to the top of the side edge as a faux fastener.

PILLOW

1 Cut two rectangles of fabric that measure 4" x 3" (10cm x 7.5cm). Using a scant ¼" seam, machine stitch all the way around leaving open a small gap for turning. Turn right side out and press, stuff lightly and close the opening.

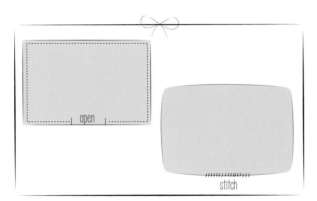

2 Measure and mark lightly with a pen two evenly spaced dots on one side of the pillow. Using four strands of contrasting embroidery thread and the dots as a guide, hand stitch right through the thickness of the pillow and back up to the top, pull the thread tight and tie off. Repeat with the remaining dot.

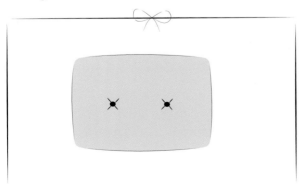

TENT TOP

1 Trace the tent pattern piece on to a large piece of paper, flip it and trace again matching the piece at the marked symbols.

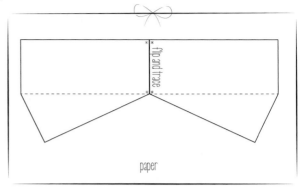

2 Fold the felt in half and place the tent pattern piece on the fold of the felt as marked and cut one. Repeat and cut another so you have two that look like this.

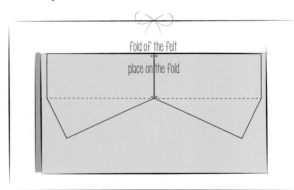

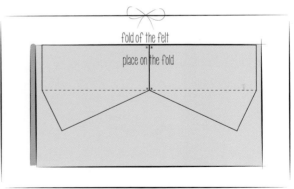

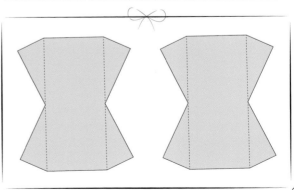

3 Cut out eight leaves from leaf green felt and four flower dots from lemon felt. Place them as shown below on one tent piece only. This will then be your tent outer layer. Machine top stitch the leaves and flowers in place.

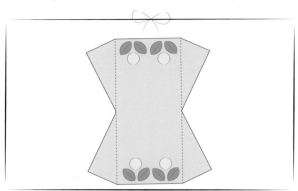

4 Trace and cut two squares of Vilene Heavy Backing that measure 7½" x 6½" (19cm x 16½"). Place them in the centre of the wrong side of the tent top as shown below and also on one side of the remaining tent piece.

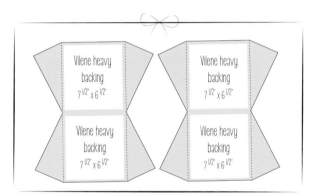

5 Place the two tent pieces together with the Vilene Heavy Backing sides facing. Cut four pieces of ribbon that measure approx. 8" (20cm) long. Pin one end of each piece of ribbon between the two tent pieces as shown below.

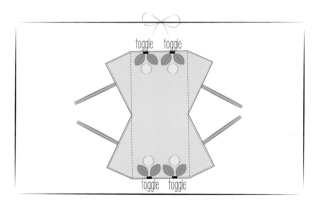

6 Using matching thread to your felt, machine top stitch all the way around the outer edge of the tent, making sure you catch the ends of the ribbon in the stitching.

7 Machine top stitch along the top of the tent.

8 Stitch a toggle button just below each set of leaves on each side of the tent front, four in total.

TENT BASE

1 Cut two pieces of felt for the base that measure 7" x 7" (18cm x 18cm). Cut two pieces of Vilene Heavy Backing that measure 6½" x 6½" (16½cm x 16½cm).

2 Cut 4 short lengths of thin black elastic measuring approx. 2½" (6cm) long each.

3 Fold each short piece in half to form a tiny loop and add a few stitches to hold. Pin each loop as shown in diagram below, with the loops hanging over the outer edge.

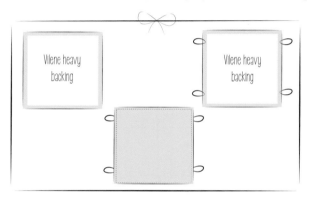

4 With wrong sides together, place the remaining base piece on top of the first one and top stitch around the outer edge through all thicknesses, making sure to catch the ends of the elastic in the stitching. Attach the base to the tent by looping the toggle button through the elastic. Knot the ends of the ribbon and use them to tie the opening flaps of the tent closed.

The Best of Friends!

Bear, Bear so big and strong, carries little Evie everywhere.

evie & the bear

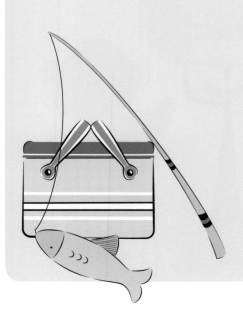

Evie measures: 13cm (5") tall - Bear measures: 30cm (12") tall

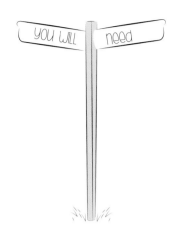
you will need

EVIE AND THE BEAR

TEMPLATES ON PAGES 107-109

- 40cm x 40cm (16"x 16") chocolate brown wool felt for bear head, body, ears and arms
- 10cm x 14cm (4"x 5 ½") cream wool felt for bear snout and fish face
- 10cm x 12cm (4"x 5") light grey wool felt for fish body
- 23cm x 30cm (9"x 12") leaf green wool felt for carry basket
- 15cm x 10cm (6"x 4") peach wool felt for doll head and arms
- 13cm x 20cm (5"x 8") white wool felt for doll body
- 12cm x 20cm (5"x 8") aqua wool felt for headscarf and fish fin
- 12cm x 5cm (8"x 2") red wool felt for collar
- 12cm x 8cm (5"x 3") sandy wool felt for doll head and hair
- x2 4mm English glass dolls eyes for doll
- x2 6mm English glass dolls eyes for bear
- Gutermann Upholstery thread for attaching the eyes

- Long doll making needle
- Sewing machine thread to match the felt
- Black embroidery thread
- x1 vintage /novelty button for doll
- x2 vintage /novelty buttons for basket
- 27cm (10 ½") long piece of 5mm wooden dowel for fishing rod
- x1 tiny metal screw eyelet for fishing rod
- 18cm (7") long piece of cotton string for fish
- Scrap lengths of Jamieson's Shetland Spindrift 4ply yarn
- 3.25mm knitting needles for scarf
- Toy fill
- General sewing supplies
- Craft glue

A very tiny seam allowance is needed and included for Evie, Bear, the fish and the carry basket. 3mm on all pieces

BEAR'S HEAD

* Head Gusset Diagrams are on page 12

1 Machine stitch around the head pieces leaving open where indicated at the base of the head, leave the dart at the back of the head open at this stage. (see fig A)

2 Position the dart at the back of the head so that the seams match, machine stitch the dart from edge to edge, turn right side out, making sure to gently ease out all the curves and the point of the snout. Stuff the head and snout until very firm with toy fill. (see fig B)

BEAR'S SNOUT COVER

1 Machine stitch around the front edge of the snout pieces as shown, leaving open where indicated.

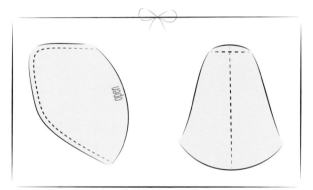

2 Bring the seams in the snout together and stitch across the tip to form the nose.

3 Place a small amount of stuffing inside the snout and place it over the nose on the head, hand stitch in place, tucking under the tiny raw edge as you stitch.

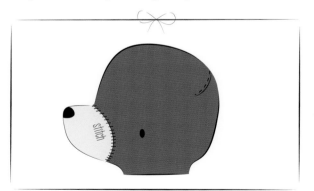

4 Using two strands of black embroidery thread, stitch a few backstitches over each other on the tip of the snout. Place a long stitch down the front of the snout. Pass the thread back through the stitches and fasten off.

BEAR'S FACE

1 Mark the position for the eyes with pins. Attach the English glass eyes per instructions on page page 11 using Gutermann Upholstery Thread to match the felt. Anchor your thread inside the stuffing in the head opening.

BEAR'S BODY

1 Machine stitch all the way around the body pieces leaving open where indicated at the top edge.

2 Turn the body right side out, making sure to gently ease out the little legs. Stuff the body until firm with toy fill.

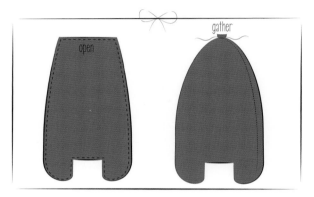

3 Gather by hand around the top edge of he body, pull up the gathers so the top edge of the body just curves in and fasten the stitches off.

4 Place the head on top of the gathered stitches in the body. Place pins in to hold the head on tight while you stitch the head on to the body.

BEAR'S ARMS

* Stitching/Attaching Arms Diagrams are on page 12

1 Stitch the arms all the way around, leaving open where indicated, turn right side out and stuff the arms firmly in the 'hands' and place less stuffing in the 'top' of the arm, close the openings on the arms. Pin the arms to each side of the body just under the head and with two strands of matching thread and a long doll making needle, stitch right through one arm through the body and out the other side of the other arm, keep going through in this fashion many times until the arms are firm, fasten off.

BEAR'S EARS

1 Machine stitch all the way around each ear leaving open where indicated, turn right side out and stitch the opening closed, making sure to tuck in a tiny raw edge as you stitch.

2 Pin the ears to the either side of the head just in front of the head dart and stitch in place using matching thread.

EVIE'S HEAD

* Stitching Doll Head and Hair Diagrams are on * (page 12) *

1 Place the hair piece on top of the peach head piece as marked. Using matching thread to the hair on your sewing machine, top stitch across the hair.

2 With right sides together, stitch around the outer edge of the head, leaving open at the bottom where indicated.

3 Turn the head right side out and stuff very firmly. The head circumference should measure approx. 16 ½cm (6 ½")

4 Mark the position for the eyes with pins. Attach the English glass eyes per instructions on page 11 using Gutermann Upholstery Thread to match the felt. Anchor your thread inside the stuffing in the head opening.

5 Using two strands of black embroidery thread, stitch a small back stitch in place as the mouth.

EVIE'S BODY

1 Machine stitch all the way around the two body pieces, leaving open where indicated at the bottom and at the side for turning.

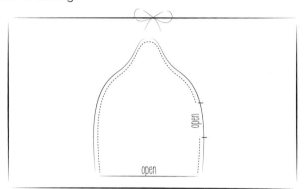

2 Machine stitch the base oval in place, turn the body right side out and stuff firmly. Stitch the opening in the side closed.

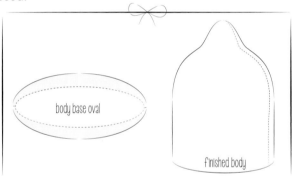

body base oval

finished body

3 Make a small indent with your finger in the opening in the head and push the neck of the body inside the head, hold the head on with pins while you stitch the head in place, tucking under the raw edge of the felt as you go.

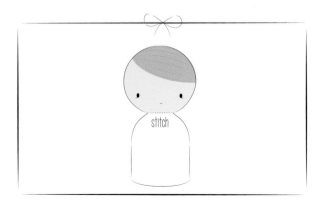

stitch

EVIE'S ARMS

* Stitching / Attaching Doll Arm Diagrams are on page 12

1 Stitch the arms all the way around, leaving open where indicated, turn right side out and place a small amount of stuffing in to the 'hands', close the openings on the arms. Pin the arms to each side of the body just under the head. With two strands of Gutermann Upholstery Thread and a long doll making needle, stitch right through one arm through the body and out the other side of the other arm, keep going through in this fashion many times until the arms are firm, fasten off. Place a few tiny stitches in the 'hands' to hold them at the front.

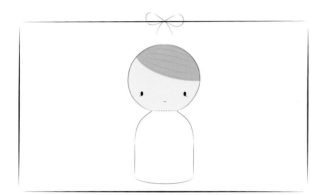

EVIE'S COLLAR

1 Wrap the collar around the neck and add a tiny stitch to the front to hold.

EVIE'S HEADSCARF

1 Wrap the headscarf around the head and place a few small dabs of craft glue just under the edge that touches the head. Bring the small ends to the front under her chin and glue them in place.

2 Add a tiny stitch to the back of the scarf to hold it down.

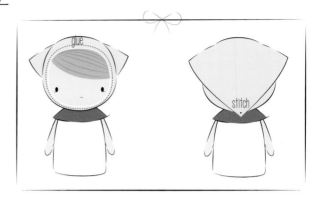

3 Tie the bow in a knot and stitch it to the front of the headscarf.

4 Stitch a small vintage/novelty button to her hair.

CARRY BASKET

1 Bring the short straight sides together on one basket piece and stitch. Machine stitch the base oval in place on the smaller end of the basket. Repeat with the remaining basket and base oval.

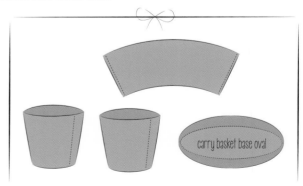

2 With right sides together, place one basket inside the other matching the seams. Machine stitch all the way around the top open edge, leaving a small gap for turning. Turn the piece right side out, and tuck one basket inside the other. Hand stitch the opening closed.

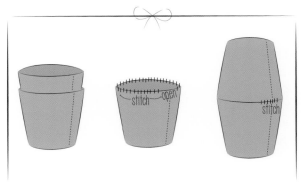

3 Cut two strips of felt for the straps that measure approx. 23cm x 3cm (9″ x 1¼″).

4 Fold them in half lengthwise and top stitch. Stitch one end of one strap to the top of the back of the basket as shown in below 15. Stitch a button in place on the strap as well, repeat with the remaining strap.

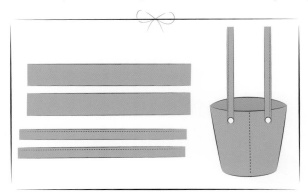

5 Place the basket on the bears back and bring the straps to the front of his body, cross them over his body and bring them to the back again. Hand stitch the end of the strap to the back of the basket.

KNITTED SCARF

* I used Jamieson's Shetland Spindrift 4 ply yarn in the following colours:

Scotch Broom - 1160
Mogit - 107
Pebble - 127
Cloud - 764
Moss - 147
Chartreuse - 365
Sholmit - 103
Flame - 271
Birch - 252

* Knot lengths of left over yarn together to make a long length, using a different colour each time. As you knit you can add more odd lengths of yarn until you reach the desired scarf length.

1 Cast on 12 stitches

2 Garter stitch until your scarf measures approx. 18″ (46cm) long.

FISH

1 Take the fin you cut and using a contrasting colour thread on your sewing machine, top stitch straight lines over the surface of the fin, Lay aside for now.

2 Stitch the curved edge of one fish face piece to the curved edge of one fish body piece. Repeat with the remaining fish face and body pieces.

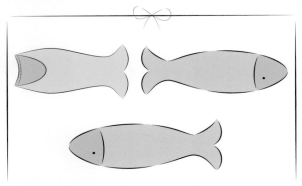

3 Using four strands of black embroidery thread, stitch a French knot in place on the right side of both face pieces as the eye.

4 Cut a piece of cotton string approx. 18cm (7") long. Place a small knot in one end. Place the two fish pieces right side together and slide the fin between the two, making sure the straight edge of the fin is in line with the side edge of the fish. Place the string inside the fish with the small knot poking out the end of the face, Stitch the fish together leaving open where indicated and making sure to catch the fin and the string in the stitching.

5 Turn right side out and stuff firmly, close the gap in the side.

FISHING POLE

Take the piece of dowel and screw the tiny eyelet in to one end. Tie the end of the string to the eyelet so your fish is hanging.

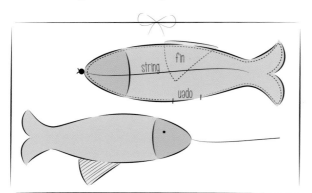

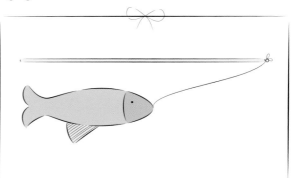

Set your paper boat afloat!

This is the life! gently rowing around the pond.

fig newton

Fig Newton measures: 15cm (6") tall - Boat measures: 20cm x 15cm (8"x 6")

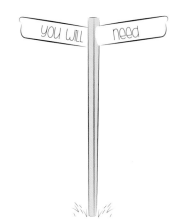

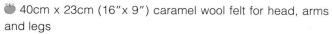

🍅 40cm x 23cm (16"x 9") caramel wool felt for head, arms and legs

🍅 20cm x 18cm (8"x 7") cream wool felt for head and body

🍅 15cm x 10cm (6"x 4") white wool felt for sailor hat brim

🍅 51cm x 30cm (20"x 12") pea green felt for boat

🍅 51cm x 12cm (20"x 5") aqua wool felt for sailor hat crown and decorative side of boat

🍅 40cm x 28cm (16"x 11") Vilene Iron On Heavy Backing for boat

🍅 13cm x 8cm (5" x 3") fabric for flag.

🍅 15cm x 10cm (6"x 4") white linen for toy 'paper' boat.

🍅 18cm x 15cm (7"x 6") light weight iron on interfacing for flag and toy 'paper' boat.

🍅 x3 4mm wide 6" (15cm) long dowel for flag and oars.

🍅 x1 wooden bead for flag.

🍅 Long piece of cotton string.

🍅 x3 vintage /novelty buttons for sailor hat and boat.

🍅 x2 8mm English glass dolls eyes.

🍅 Gutermann Upholstery thread for attaching the eyes

🍅 Long doll making needle

🍅 Jamieson's Shetland Spindrift 4ply yarn colour - Sholmit 103

🍅 3mm knitting needles for cowl

🍅 Sewing machine thread to match the felt

🍅 Black embroidery thread

🍅 Green embroidery thread

🍅 Toy fill

🍅 General sewing supplies

A very tiny seam allowance is needed and is included for fig newton. 3mm on all pieces
A scant 1/4" seam allowance is used for the sailboat and is also included

HEAD

1 Cut one head front from caramel felt and one from cream felt. Place them together and stitch along the curved edge as shown in below.

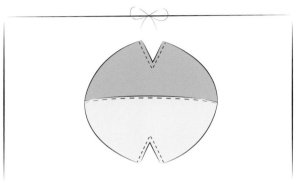

2 Open out the piece, fold in half lengthwise and stitch along the two darts at the top and bottom of the head front. Lay aside for now.

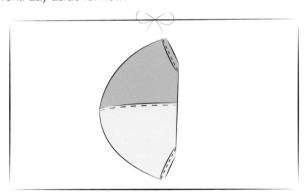

3 Take the head back piece and fold in half lengthwise and stitch along the two darts at the top and bottom of the head back.

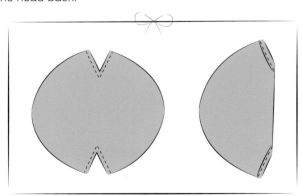

4 With right sides together, and with the caramel side of the head front uppermost, stitch all the way around the head pieces, leaving open where indicated at the bottom of the head. Turn right side out and stuff the head until it is very firm.

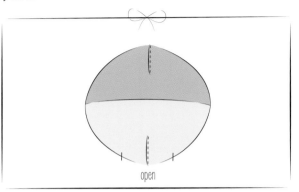

5 Mark the position for the eyes with pins. Attach the English glass eyes per instructions on page 11 using Gutermann Upholstery Thread to match the felt. Anchor your thread inside the stuffing in the head opening.

6 Using two strand of black embroidery thread, stitch a long back stitch in the seam at the front of the head as a mouth, stitch two tiny back stitches at either end of the long back stitch.

BODY

* Body Gusset Diagrams are on page 12

1 Machine stitch all the way around the body pieces leaving open where indicated at the back, leave the dart at the base of the body open at this stage. (see fig A)

2 Position the dart at the base of the body so that the seams come together, machine stitch the dart from edge to edge, turn right side out through the opening in the back, making sure to gently ease out all the curves and points. Stuff the body until very firm with toy fill. (see fig B)

3 Make a little hollow in the stuffing in the head and push the top of the body inside the head opening quite firmly, making sure the neat seam on the front of the body lines up with the front of the head. Place pins in to hold tight while you stitch the head on to the body, stuff a little more as you stitch if needed so the head is firmly attached.

LEGS

1 Cut out four legs from matching felt. Place two legs together and stitch all the way around the leg and foot leaving open where indicated at the side of the leg.

2 Turn right side out and machine stitch across the 'ankle'. Top stitch two lines of stitching on top of the foot as shown.

3 Stuff the bottom half of the leg and machine stitch across the middle of the leg to form the 'knee', leave the upper leg unstuffed. Hand stitch the leg closed tucking in the raw edge as you stitch. Repeat with the remaining leg.

4 Fold the leg at the 'knee' and add a few stitches to hold in place as shown.

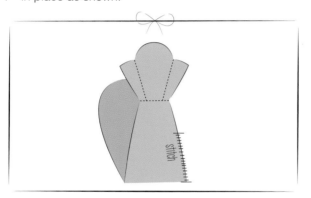

5 Pin the upper part of each leg in place on each side of the body, with the 'knees' facing forward. With two strands of matching thread and a long doll making needle, stitch right through one leg through the body and out the other side of the other leg, keep going through in this fashion many times until the legs are firm, fasten off.

ARMS

1 Stitch the arms all the way around, leaving open where indicated, turn right side out. As with the feet, machine top stitch across the 'wrist' and top stitch two lines of stitching on top of the 'hand', the arms remain unstuffed. Close the openings in the arms. Pin the arms to each side of the body just under the head and with two strands of matching thread and a long doll making needle, stitch right through one arm through the body and out the other side of the other arm, keep going through in this fashion many times until the arms are firm, fasten off.

KNITTED COWL

* I used Jamieson's Shetland Spindrift 4 ply yarn colour: Sholmit 103

Cast on 100 stitches

Work in seed stitch

1 Knit 1, purl 1 to the end of the row.

2 Purl 1, knit 1, to the end of the row.

Repeat 1st and 2nd row until you have knitted 10 rows.

Cast off and weave in the ends of the yarn.

3 Begin at the back of the neck, bring the cowl around the front of the body, cross it over at the front, tuck it under the arms and back around the back of the body. Stitch the ends neatly together at the back of the body.

SAILOR HAT

1 Take the two sailor hat crown pieces and stitch them around the curved edge. Leaving the straight edge open. Turn right side out.

2 Take the two sailor hat brims, stitch them together along the top curved edge. Open it out and with right sides together, stitch the two short ends together.

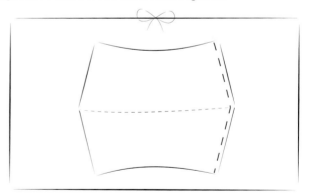

3 With right sides together, slide the hat crown inside the brim and using match embroidery thread, hand stitch the open edge of the crown to one of the raw edges of the brim. Fold the remaining open edge of the brim down.

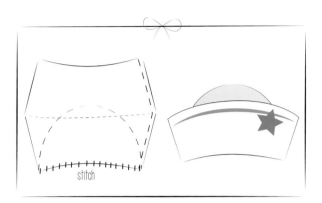

4 Using the green embroidery thread, stitch a long back stitch in place around the top outer edge of the sailor hat as decoration, stitch a vintage/novelty button to one side of the front of the sailor hat.

5 Stuff the crown with a small amount of stuffing, place the hat on top of the head slightly to the right. Stitch in place tucking under a tiny raw edge as you stitch.

ROW BOAT

1 Iron the Vilene Heavy Backing pieces in place as shown in below, to the back of the two boat base pieces.

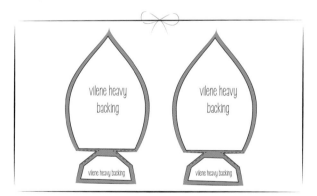

2 With right sides together, bring the dart corners of the boat base together and machine stitch. Repeat with the remaining boat base.

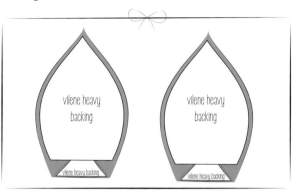

3 With wrong sides facing, place the two boat base pieces together, and machine top stitch all the way around the outer edge.

4 Cut out two boat side pieces on the fold of the felt. Cut out one boat side decorative piece on the fold of the felt. Place the decorative side piece along one straight edge of one boat side piece and top stitch in place. Stitch a long piece of decorative ribbon in place along the top edge of the decorative side piece.

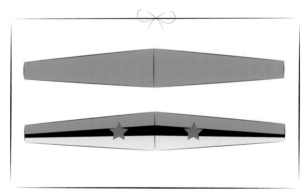

5 Iron the Vilene Heavy Backing pieces as shown in below, to the back of the two boat sides. With wrong sides facing, place the two boat side pieces together, and machine top stitch all the way around the outer edge.

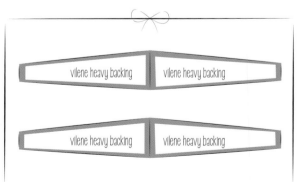

6 Hand stitch the boat side to the boat base around the curved edge of the boat base. Starting at the short straight edge at the back and bringing it around the pointed front and back around to the short end at the back to finish. Stitch a vintage/novelty button in place on the side of the boat close to the front pointed end of the boat.

7 Take a long piece of cotton string and stitch it in place around the top edge of the boat, making loops as you go, fasten off .

FLAG

1 Glue one end of the dowel inside the bead and allow to dry.

2 Cut a rectangle of fabric and light interfacing that measure approx. 5" x 3" (13cm x 8cm). Iron the interfacing to the back of the fabric. Pin the pattern piece to the fabric and cut out the flag.

3 Place a generous amount of craft glue to the interfacing side of the fabric and wrap the flag around the dowel so the centre of the flag wraps around the dowel. Bring the pointy ends of the flag together and press them firmly until the glue dries.

4 Place the end of the flagpole inside the boat at the back with the flag pointing outside the boat. Add a few stitches around the flagpole to attach it to the back of the boat.

TOY 'PAPER' BOAT

* Cut a piece of white linen and light interfacing that measure 4" x 6" (10cm x 15cm). Press the interfacing to one side of the linen.

1 With linen side of the piece uppermost, fold it in half and press.

2 Fold the piece in half again the other way and press.

3 Open out the last fold you did and use the crease as a guide to fold down the sides in to a triangle.

4 Fold up one bottom straight edge, turn the piece over and fold up the remaining straight edge and press.

5 Open the piece out and squash it down so you have a diamond shape and press.

6 Fold up one pointed end to form a small triangle, turn the piece over and fold up the remaining pointed end and press.

7 Open the piece out and squash it down so you have a diamond shape and press.

8 Carefully pull the sides outwards, folding the pointed middle so it lies flat and press.

9 Tuck under the tiny triangles that are inside the boat, place a few stitches on the outer ends to hold the piece in place.

OARS

1 Cut a piece of grey felt that measures approx. 6" x 5" (15cm x 13cm) and a piece of green felt that measures 6" x 2" (15cm x 5cm).

2 Stitch the two pieces together along the longest side, open out and press lightly.

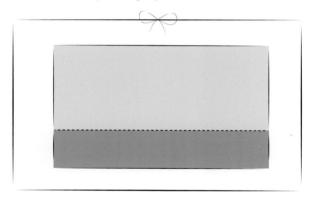

3 Pin the oar pattern piece so that the placement line matches the seam in the felt. Making sure that the end of the oar is on the green half of the felt. Cut out four oars in this manner.

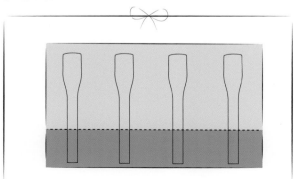

4 Place two oars together and top stitch all the way around, leaving open at the tiny short end. Top stitch down the paddle end to form a channel for the dowel to fit in.

5 Slide the dowel inside each oar and machine top stitch across the end to close.

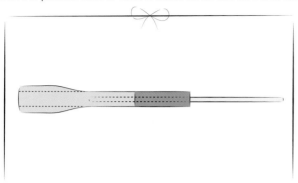

Fig Newton Toy Paper Boat Folding Diagrams

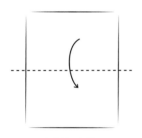

1. fold in half

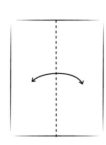

2. fold in half again

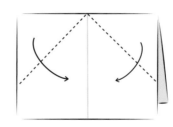

3. fold in corners to from a triangle

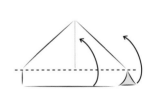

4. fold up the edges on both sides

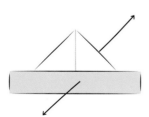

5. pull the sides out and flatten

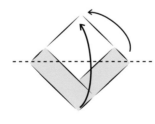

6. fold front and back layers up

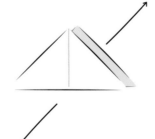

7. Pull sides apart and flatten to form a diamond shape

8. Pull the sides out wards

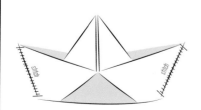

9. Place a few stitches to hold

The air is Crisp!

Autumn is here, load your pack, time to set off......
Dress up warmly Mr. Oak

mr. oak

⋈

Mr. Oak measures: 33cm (13") tall

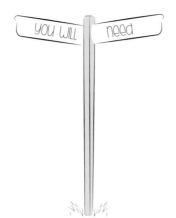
you will need

MR. OAK

TEMPLATES ON PAGES 113–117

- 47cm x 42cm (18½"x 16½") rusty orange wool felt for fox head, body, tail, arms and legs
- 42cm x 36cm (18½"x 14") pea green wool felt for jacket
- 46cm x 23cm (18"x 9") light grey wool felt for beret and sash
- 38cm x 5cm (15"x 2") white wool felt for cravat
- 42cm x 10cm (16½"x 4") charcoal grey wool felt for boots and ears
- 28cm x 8cm (11"x 3") cream wool felt for tail tip and ears
- 5cm x 5cm (2"x 2") black wool felt for nose
- 36cm x 7cm (14"x 3") fabric for jacket collar
- 25cm x 23cm (10"x 9") linen for back pack
- 25cm x 23cm (10"x 9") fabric for back pack
- 33cm (13") velvet ribbon for beret
- x4 small pea green pom poms
- x2 6mm English glass dolls eyes

- Gutermann Upholstery thread for attaching the eyes
- Long doll making needle
- Sewing machine thread to match the felt
- Black embroidery thread
- x1 vintage /novelty button for back pack
- 1" bias tape maker
- Toy fill
- General sewing supplies

A very tiny seam allowance is needed and is included for mr. oak, 3mm on all pieces.
A scant 1/4" seam allowance is used for the jacket and is also included.

HEAD

* Head Gusset Diagrams are on page 12

1 Machine stitch around the head pieces leaving open where indicated at the base of the head. Leave the dart at the back of the head open at this stage. (see fig A)

2 Position the dart at the back of the head so that the seams match, machine stitch the dart from edge to edge, turn right side out, making sure to gently ease out all the curves and the point of the snout. Stuff the head until very firm with toy fill.
(see fig B)

3 Mark the position for the eyes with pins. Attach the English glass eyes per instructions on page page 11 using Gutermann Upholstery Thread to match the felt. Anchor your thread inside the stuffing in the head opening.

4 Cut out one nose from black felt. Fold the piece in half and stitch the gusset from fold to edge.

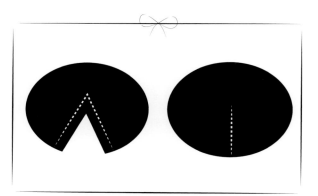

5 Pin the nose to the end of the snout with the gusset seam at the bottom and stitch in place tucking under the tiny raw outer edge as you stitch.

6 Using two strands of black embroidery thread, stitch a long back stitch in place along the seam under the snout.

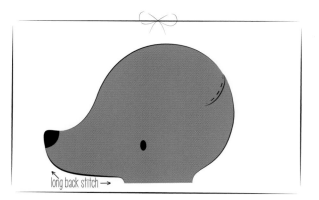

long back stitch →

BODY

* Body Gusset Diagrams are on page 12

1 Use the same body as Thistle. Machine stitch all the way around the body pieces leaving open where indicated at the back, leave the dart at the base of the body open at this stage. (see fig A)

2 Position the dart at the base of the body so that the seams come together, machine stitch the dart from edge to edge, turn right side out through the opening in the back, making sure to gently ease out all the curves and points. Stuff the body until very firm with toy fill. (see fig B)

3 Make a little hollow in the stuffing in the head and push the top of the body inside the head opening quite firmly, making sure the neat seam on the front of the body lines up with the front of the head. Place pins in to hold tight while you stitch the head on to the body, stuff a little more as you stitch if needed so the head is firmly attached.

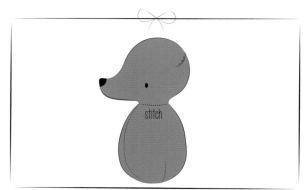

stitch

LEGS

* Stitching/Attaching Leg Diagrams are on page 12

1 Cut out four legs from matching felt. Place two legs together and stitch all the way around the leg and foot leaving open where indicated at the back of the leg. Turn right side out and stuff the whole leg well. Hand stitch the leg closed tucking in the raw edge as you stitch. Repeat with the remaining leg.

2 Pin the legs in place on each side of the body, and with two strands of matching thread and a long doll making needle, stitch right through one leg through the body and out the other side of the other leg, keep going through in this fashion many times until the legs are firm, fasten off.

ARMS

* Stitching/Attaching Arm Diagrams are on page 12

1 Stitch the arms all the way around, leaving open where indicated, turn right side out and stuff the arms firmly, close the openings on the arms. Pin the arms to each side of the body just under the head and with two strands of matching thread and a long doll making needle, stitch right through one arm through the body and out the other side of the other arm, keep going through in this fashion many times until the arms are firm, fasten off.

TAIL

1 Place the tail tip on top of one of the tail pieces making sure the point of the tail tip lines up with the point of the tail.

2 Machine top stitch it in place along the curved top edge. Repeat with the remaining tail tip and tail piece but this time make sure you do it in reverse.

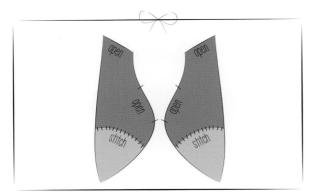

3 With right sides together, stitch all the way around the tail, leaving open where indicated. Turn right side out through the opening in the side of the tail.

4 Stuff the tail well and close the opening in the side of the tail. Stitch the tail to the base of the body, tucking under the tiny raw edge as you stitch.

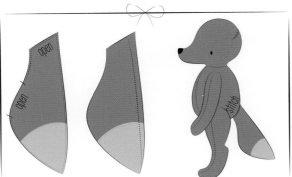

BOOTS

1 Stitch the boots all the way around, leaving open where indicated at the top. Turn the boot right side out and slide it on to the foot. Repeat with the other boot pieces.

CRAVAT

1 Cut a piece of white wool felt approx. 15"x 2" (38cm x 5cm) wrap it around the neck and tie at the front.

BERET

1 On a large piece of paper, trace the beret pattern piece one next to the other six times until you have a pointy crown shape as illustrated in below. Cut one of these from wool felt. Top stitch the length of ribbon along the bottom curved edge.

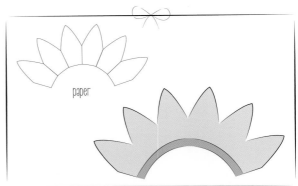

2 With right sides together, stitch all the points, one to the other all the way around. The last one will be the back seam.

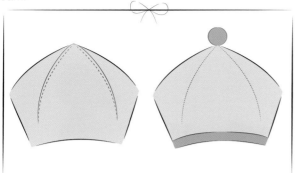

3 Turn the beret right side out and press all the seams. Stitch a pom pom to the top. Place the beret on to Mr. Oak's head; making sure the back seam is at the back of his head. Tilt the top of the beret to one side.

EARS

1 Cut two ears from charcoal grey and two from cream wool felt. Place them together in pairs each pair having one charcoal grey one cream colour ear. Machine stitch all the way around each ear leaving open where indicated, turn right side out and stitch the opening closed, making sure to tuck in a tiny raw edge as you stitch.

2 Pin the ears to the top of the beret with the grey side of each ear at the back of the head. Slightly curve the ears as you stitch them in place through the beret and the head.

JACKET

1 With right sides together, stitch the centre back seam of the jacket back. Open out the jacket back.

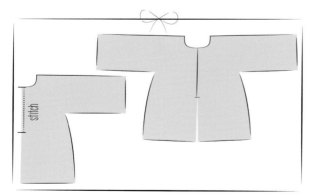

2 With right sides together, place one jacket front on top of the jacket back matching shoulder seams, stitch the shoulder seam. Repeat with remaining jacket front and shoulder seam.

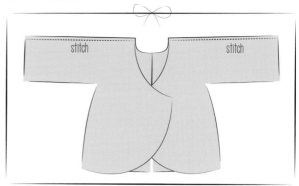

COLLAR

1 Place the collar on the fold and cut one from wool felt and one from fabric. With right sides together, stitch the collar along the curved edge, clip, turn right side out and press.

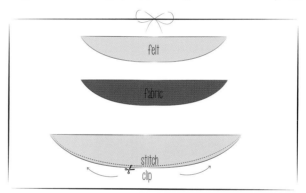

2 Open out the jacket so it lies flat, wrong side up. Pin the raw edge of the collar fabric side up to the top edge of the jacket. Stitch in place through all thicknesses.

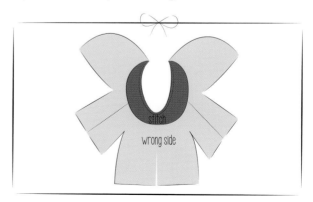

3 With right sides together, stitch along the under side of the sleeve seam and down the side seam, repeat on the other side. Make a tiny snip where the sleeve and the side seam meet. Turn right side out.

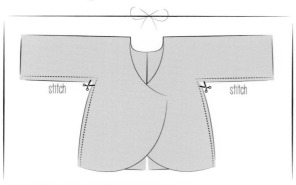

4 Place the jacket on to Mr. Oak and roll the collar down. Bring one side of the front of the jacket across the other and overlap, add a few stitches to hold it in place.

SASH

1 Cut a piece of wool felt approx. 18"x 1" (46cm x 2½") long.

2 Gather by hand, each end of the sash and stitch a pom pom in place on each end of the sash.

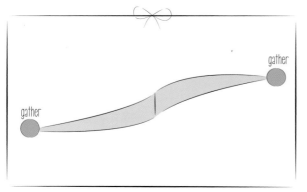

3 Wrap the sash around the tummy, just under the arms and tie it in place at the front.

BACK PACK

1 On a large piece of paper, trace around the satchel pattern piece on page 126. On one of the rectangular ends of the satchel pattern, extend it by drawing an extra 2½" (6½cm) this will become the closing flap. From this new pattern cut one from linen and one from fabric.

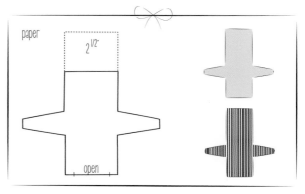

2 With right sides together, stitch all the way around the back pack, leaving open where indicated at the shorter end.

3 Clip the corners and curves and turn the piece right side out and press. Hand stitch the opening closed.

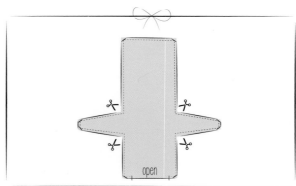

3 Bring together one side with the shorter rectangular end and hand stitch them together, repeat with the remaining side.

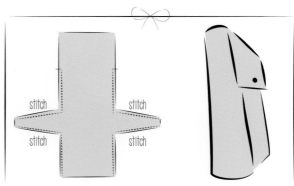

4 Using a 1" bias tape maker, make the following for the back pack straps:
x2 pieces that measures: - 1½"x 7½" (4cm x 19cm) long.

5 Tuck in the raw ends and top stitch each strap. Hand stitch one end of each strap to the top of the back of the back pack. Stitch the remaining end of both straps to the bottom of the back of the back pack.

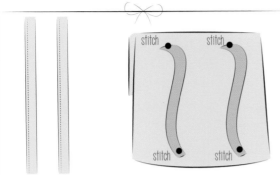

6 Stitch a vintage/novelty button to the front flap and hang the back pack over both shoulders.

How splendid you look Purslane!

your knitted beret is lovely! ...
perfect for sledging.

purslane

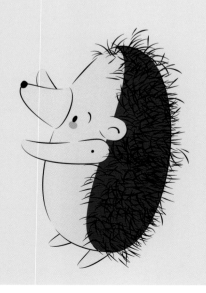

Purslane measures: 13cm (5") tall - Sleigh measures: 18cm x 10cm (7"x 4")

- 🍎 40cm x 15cm (16"x 6") cream felt for body, ears, arms, legs and snout
- 🍎 15cm x 13cm (6"x 5") hedgehog fur fabric for body
- 🍎 42cm x 24cm (16½"x 9½") caramel felt for sleigh and apple leaf
- 🍎 36cm x 30cm (14"x 12") charcoal grey felt for sleigh skis
- 🍎 50cm x 40cm (20"x 16") Vilene Iron on Heavy Backing for sleigh
- 🍎 Toy fill
- 🍎 x1 3½cm (9") pom pom for apple
- 🍎 x2 vintage/novelty buttons for sleigh
- 🍎 x2 4mm English glass dolls eyes
- 🍎 Gutermann Upholstery thread for attaching the eyes
- 🍎 Long doll making needle
- 🍎 Sewing machine thread to match the felt
- 🍎 Brown Perle cotton

- 🍎 Charcoal grey embroidery thread for attaching skis
- 🍎 Black embroidery thread for nose
- 🍎 Jamieson's Shetland Spindrift 4ply yarn in Moss 147 and Cloud 764
- 🍎 2.75mm knitting needles for beret
- 🍎 3.25mm knitting needles for blanket
- 🍎 General sewing supplies
- 🍎 Craft glue

A very tiny seam allowance is needed and is included for purslane, 3mm on all pieces. A scant 1/4" seam allowance is used for the sleigh.

HEDGEHOG

1 Bring the dart edges together in the felt body piece and stitch along this edge. With right sides together, repeat with the remaining dart in the hedgehog fur body piece.

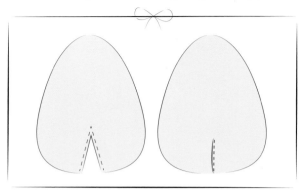

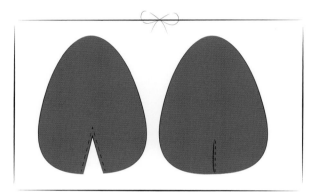

2 Place both body pieces right sides together, stitch all the way around the body, leaving open where indicated in the side seam and making sure the dart seams match. Turn right side out and stuff the body firmly. Hand stitch the opening closed.

3 Using a large needle, gently ease out the tiny fronds of fur from between the stitches.

SNOUT

1 Fold the piece together so the straight edges meet. Machine stitch along this straight edge, turn right side out and stuff, making sure to get small pieces of stuffing in to the tiny end of the snout.

2 Pin the snout to the felt side of the body approx. 1¼" (3cm) down from the top of the head. Hand stitch it in place tucking under the raw edge as you stitch.

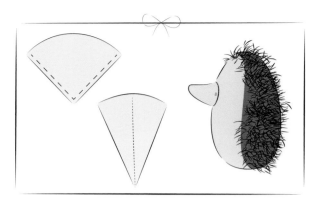

FACE

1 Mark the position for the eyes with pins. Attach the English glass eyes per instructions on page 11 using Gutermann Upholstery Thread to match the felt. Anchor your thread just under the edge of the snout.

2 Using two strands of black embroidery thread, stitch a few backstitches over each other on the tip of the snout. Pass the thread back through the stitches and fasten off.

EARS

1 Machine stitch all the way around each ear leaving open where indicated, turn right side out.

2 Make a little fold in the straight end of each ear and hold with a small stitch. Pin each ear to the side of the head in line with the eyes and stitch in place, tucking under the raw edge as you stitch.

ARMS

1 Stitch the arms all the way around, leaving open where indicated, turn right side out and stuff the arms firmly in the 'hands' and place less stuffing in the 'top' of the arm, close the openings on the arms.

2 Pin the arms to each side of the body just under the ears and with two strands of matching thread and a long doll making needle, stitch right through one arm through the body and out the other side of the other arm, keep going through in this fashion many times until the arms are firm, fasten off page 12.

3 Bring the hands together at the front of the body; add a few stitches to hold them together.

FEET

1 Stitch the feet all the way around, leaving open where indicated, turn right side out and stuff the feet firmly.

2 Pin the back round end of the feet to the under side of the body approx. 2" (5cm) apart. Bring the pointy toes together at the front and add a few stitches to hold them together.

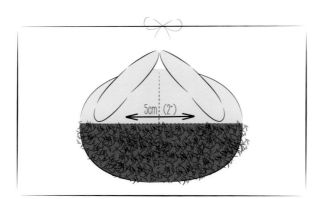

KNITTED BERET

* I used Jamieson's Shetland Spindrift 4 ply yarn in:

- Moss 147   - Beret
- Cloud 764   - Pom Pom

BERET

Using 3.25mm knitting needles, cast on 40 stitches

1 Knit 1, Purl 1 for 5 rows

2 Increase in to every stitch - 80 stitches

3 Beginning with a Purl row stocking stitch 5 rows.

DECREASING

1st row knit 6, knit 2together to the end - 70 stitches 2nd row purl

3rd row knit 5, knit 2 together to the end - 60 stitches.

4th row purl

5th row knit 4, knit 2 together to the end - 50 stitches.

6th row purl.

7th row knit 3, knit 2 together to the end - 40 stitches.

8th row purl.

9th knit 2, knit 2 together to the end - 30 stitches.

10th row purl.

11th row knit 1, knit 2 together to the end - 20 stitches.

12th row purl.

13th row knit 2 together to the end - 10 stitches.

Cut the yarn from the ball leaving a long tail. Thread the yarn tail on to a large bodkin and thread it through the remaining 10 stitches on the knitting needle, pulling the knitting needle out. Pull up the stitches tightly and fasten off (don't cut the yarn yet). Stitch the row ends of the beret together. Weave the ends of the yarn in.

POM POM

Cast on 7 stitches

1st row purl.

2nd Increase in every stitch - 14 stitches.

3rd Beginning with a purl row, stocking stitch 5 rows.

4th Knit 2 together to the end.

5 Cut the yarn from the ball leaving a long tail. Thread the yarn tail on to a large bodkin and thread it through the 14 stitches on the knitting needle, pulling the knitting needle out and pulling the stitches tight.

6 Stitch the row ends together and stuff the pom pom well. Gather around the opening, pull up the gathers and fasten off. Stitch the pom pom to the beret.

KNITTED BLANKET

* I used Jamieson's Shetland Spindrift 4 ply yarn in: Cloud 764

Using 3.25mm knitting needles, cast on 64 stitches

1st Knit 2, Purl 2 to the end of the row.

2nd Repeat this pattern until you have knitted 30 rows.

Cast off

BLOCKING THE KNITTED BLANKET

* Blocking the knitted blanket is important. It will help to even out the stitches and help the blanket to hold its shape and lie flat. This process is steam blocking.

1 Pin the blanket right side down on to your ironing board. Steel head pins are best for this.

2 Place a damp cloth over the top of the blanket and using the hottest steam setting on your iron, press the cloth so the steam is pushed through the blanket. Keep going in this fashion until the cloth is almost dry.

3 Remove the cloth and leave the blanket pinned in place until it is very dry. Remove pins and your blanket is ready to go.

SLEIGH

1 Take the Vilene Heavy Backing pieces you cut and place them on to the felt sleigh pieces. Iron them in place with a dry iron until they stick.

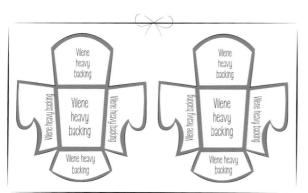

2 With wrong sides together, place the two felt sleigh pieces together and machine top stitch all the way around.

3 Bring up the back rest edges to meet the edges of the two sides and hand stitch them in place using a matching thread to the felt. Now bring the front edges up to meet the remaining side edges, hand stitch them in place.

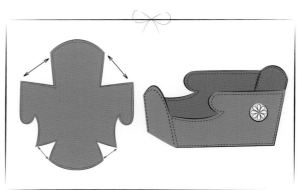

4 Stitch a vintage/decorative button to both sides of the sleigh. Set the sleigh aside for now.

SLEIGH SKIS

1 Take the Vilene Heavy Backing pieces you cut and place them on to the felt ski pieces, iron them in place with a dry iron until they stick.

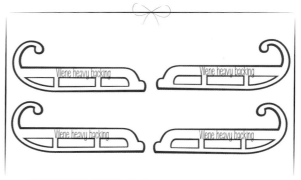

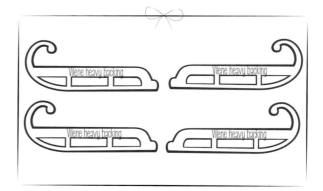

2 With wrong sides facing, place two skis together and machine top stitch around the whole shape using matching thread. Repeat until you have four matching skis.

3 Using a strong craft glue stick the four skis together in two groups. Place a heavy book on top of them and allow to dry, this may take a few hours.

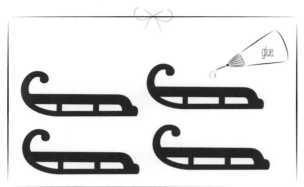

4 Once dry, and making sure the curved end of each ski is facing forward. Take one set of skis and tie it to one side of the sleigh by threading a long needle with four strands of thread. Push the needle through the ski out through the side of the sleigh and back out through the ski again; Tie a knot in the thread so it is tight, trim the thread. Repeat this process until you have three ties holding the ski to the sleigh. Repeat with the remaining ski on the other side of the sleigh.

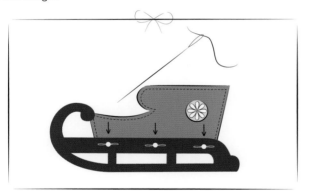

APPLE

1 Take a 3½ cm pom pom. Thread a long needle with a long length of brown Perle cotton.

2 Place a large knot in the end and push the needle right up through the pom pom. Keep going through a few times, pulling it firm to form the apple shape.

3 On the last time through leave a small loop at the top of the apple to form a 'stalk', fasten off.

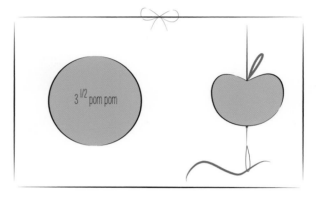

4 Take the leaf shapes you cut and machine stitch around the outer edge. Leaving open where indicated on the side. Clip ends and turn right side out. Hand stitch the opening closed.

5 Machine top stitch 'veins' in a contrasting colour.

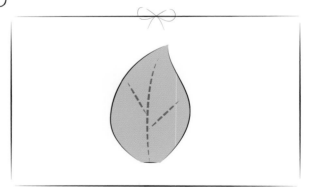

6 Stitch one end of the leaf to the top of the apple next to the loop.

Waiting for the Post!

What will it be today snail?

a postcard from somewhere far away,

or a letter from your true love.

snail mail

Snail measures: 13cm (5") long - Mailbox measures: 14cm x 10cm (5.5"x 4")

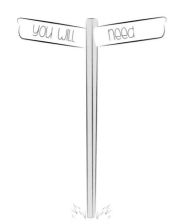
you will need

SNAIL MAIL

TEMPLATES ON PAGES 121-122

SNAIL

🍎 7"x 6" (18cm x 15cm) aqua wool felt for body
🍎 9" x 7" (23cm x 18cm) caramel wool felt for shell
🍎 8" (20cm) long piece of black 20 gauge craft wire for antenna and glasses
🍎 x2 3mm English glass dolls eyes
🍎 Gutermann Upholstery Thread for attaching the eyes
🍎 Sewing machine and embroidery thread to match the felt
🍎 Toy fill
🍎 Small pair of round nose pliers

ENVELOPE AND LETTER

🍎 14"x 7" (36cm x 18cm) white linen for the envelope
🍎 14" x 7" (36cm x 18cm) light weight iron on interfacing for the envelope
🍎 Small piece of Vlisofix
🍎 Small scrap of fabric for the stamp
🍎 Black embroidery thread
🍎 Vintage/novelty button for stamp
🍎 White sewing machine thread
🍎 7½"x 3" (19cm x 8cm) linen for the letter
🍎 7½"x 3" (19cm x 8cm) light weight iron on interfacing for the letter
🍎 Small scraps of yellow, leaf green and brown wool felt for the flower
🍎 Sewing machine thread to match the linen and felt.

MAILBOX

🍎 Large piece of paper approx. 17" x 12" (43cm x 30cm) for pattern
🍎 30" x 17" (76cm x 43cm) wool felt for main piece
🍎 20" x 17" (51cm x 43cm) Vilene Heavy Backing for main piece and flag
🍎 Small scrap of Vlisofix and fabric for 'MAIL'
🍎 6"x 5" (15cm x 13cm) aqua wool felt for flag
🍎 Small scrap of black wool felt for flag cover piece
🍎 5¾"x 3" (15cm x 8cm) fabric and light weight iron on interfacing for handle
🍎 6" (15cm) long piece of thin black elastic
🍎 x2 vintage/novelty buttons
🍎 Sewing machine and embroidery thread to match the felt
🍎 General sewing supplies

Mail
... X X

A very tiny seam allowance is needed and included for the snail, 3mm on all pieces
A scant 1/4" seam allowance is used for the mailbox, letter and envelope

SNAIL BODY

1 Bring the dart edges together in one body piece and stitch along this edge. Repeat with the remaining body piece, making sure you stitch the dart on this piece in reverse, so the neat side of the seam matches the neat side of the seam in the first dart.

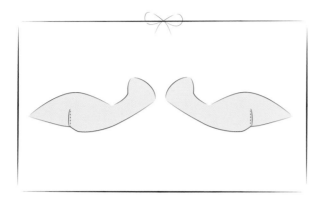

2 Place both body pieces right sides together, stitch all the way around the body, leaving open where indicated and making sure the dart seams match. Turn right side out and stuff the body firmly. Hand stitch the opening closed.

3 Angle the neck up a little and add a few stitches to hold it in place.

FACE

1 Mark the position for the eyes with pins. Attach the English glass eyes per instructions on page 11 using Gutermann Upholstery Thread to match the felt. Anchor your thread at the back of the head.

SHELL

1 Take the two shell pieces and place them together, machine stitch all the way around the shell, leaving open where indicated. Turn right side out, gently pushing the tiny end right through. Stuff the shell until quite firm.

2 Thread a needle with matching thread to the felt. Beginning at the small end, coil the shell quite firmly adding tiny stitches to hold as you coil it.

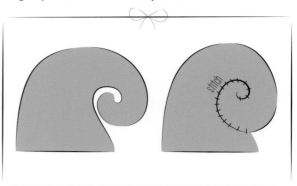

3 Place the shell on to the snail's back making sure the coiled end of the shell is facing the back. Hand stitch the shell to the body turning under a tiny raw edge as you stitch.

ANTENNA

1 Cut a piece of black wire that measures approx. 3″ (8cm) long. Take the round nose pliers and using the small round end of the pliers as a guide, make two tiny loops on either end of the wire.

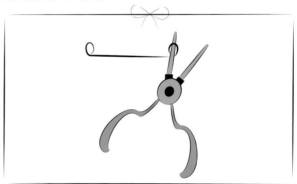

2 Now bend the wire approx. in the middle to form a 'V' shape. Using black embroidery thread, stitch the antenna to the top of the head.

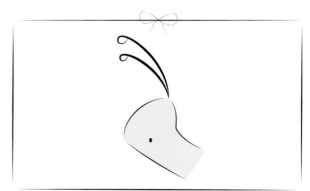

GLASSES

1 Cut a piece of wire that measures approx. 5" (12cm) long. Approx. 2" (5cm) in from one end, use the fattest end of the round nose pliers as a guide to make a circle.

2 Leave approx. 1" (2½"cm) then make another circle in the same way.

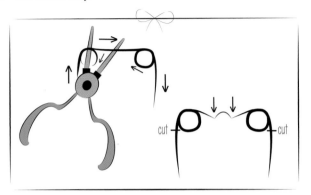

3 Now use the pliers to make a small curve in the centre of the two circles, then bend a tiny corner on either side of the middle curve to finish off the 'nose section' of the glasses. Trim the long ends of the wire off.

4 Place the glasses on to the tip of the 'nose' of the snail and add a few stitches with black embroidery thread to hold.

ENVELOPE

1 Cut a piece of linen and a piece of light iron on interfacing approx. 7" x 14" (18cm x 36cm). Iron the interfacing to one side of the linen.

2 With right sides together, fold the piece in half and trace the envelope shape to one of the interfacing sides. Mark the opening.

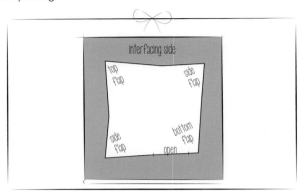

3 Machine stitch all the way around the envelope, leaving open where indicated. Trim the envelope all the way around so you are left with a scant ¼" seam allowance. Clip the corners, turn right side out, press and hand stitch the opening closed.

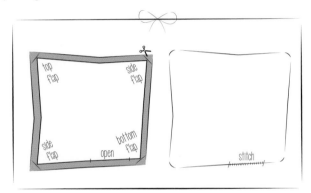

4 Fold up the bottom flap and the two side flaps so they meet (but don't overlap) in the centre, press well. (do not stitch yet) let them open out again.

5 Trace one stamp piece on to the paper side of the Vlisofix, Iron the traced shape to the wrong side of the chosen stamp fabric, cut out, remove the paper backing and press it well, in place on to the front of the envelope. Top stitch the stamp in place. Using black embroidery thread, stitch two 'X' as kisses and three dots as shown on the front of the envelope. Stitch a novelty button in place on top of the stamp.

6 Now fold up the bottom and two side edges of the envelope again and hand stitch them in place.

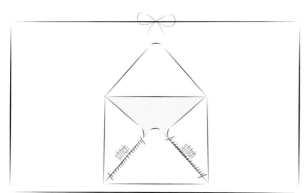

LETTER

1 Cut a piece of linen and light weight iron on interfacing 3" x 7½" (7½cm x19cm). Iron the interfacing to one side of the linen and cut the linen in half so you have two pieces measuring 3" x 3¾".

2 Cut out one circle, one stem and two leaves from felt and position them in the centre on the right side of one of the linen pieces. Machine stitch the flower pieces in place using matching thread.

3 With wrong sides together, top stitch the remaining linen piece to the back of the appliqued piece. Slide your letter in to the envelope, fold down the flap and tuck in to hold.

MAILBOX

1 Cut a rectangle of paper to measure 15½"x 5". Trace two flap pieces on to paper and cut them out. Now line up the straight edges of the two flap pieces with the top side edge of the rectangle and stick them in place (do not overlap) with sticky tape. Pin the paper pattern you have made on to the felt and cut out two.

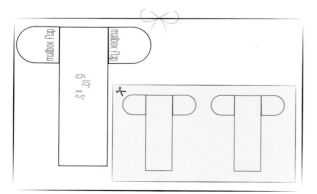

2 Trace the letters for 'MAIL' on to the paper side of the Vlisofix and cut them out roughly. (The 'L' is in reverse so when you iron it in place it will be the correct way around.)

3 Iron the letters on to the wrong side of the chosen fabric and cut them out very neatly. Peel the paper backing off, lay them in order on top of one mailbox flap and iron them in place. Top stitch each letter in place. Lay aside for now.

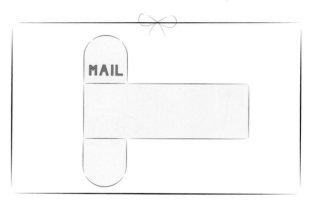

HANDLE

1 Cut a piece of fabric and light weight iron on interfacing 5¾"x 3" (14½"x 8cm). Iron the interfacing to the wrong side of the fabric.

2 With right sides together, fold the fabric in half lengthwise and stitch, leaving open a small gap along the side edge for turning. Clip the corners, turn right side out and press. Close the opening.

3 Measure up 5¾" from the bottom straight edge of the main mailbox piece. This will be your guide to placing the handle. Machine stitch the handle in place making sure that each end of the handle in approx. ½" in from the side edge of the mailbox main piece.

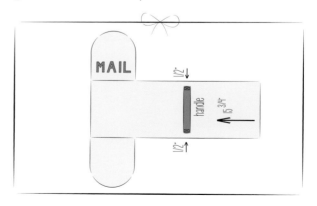

FLAG

1 Cut out two flag shapes from felt, trace and cut two flag template pieces on the Vilene Heavy Backing.

2 Making sure your felt flags are facing each other, iron the heavy backing to the back of them both. With wrong sides of the flags facing, machine top stitch around the outer edge.

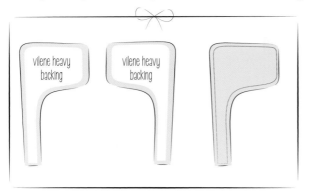

3 Pin the flag in place as shown in the diagram and add a few stitches to hold. Cut out one flag cover piece from felt and machine top stitch it in place over the end of the flag to keep it secure.

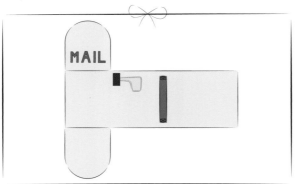

4 Cut the following from the Vilene Heavy Backing for the mailbox main piece:
- 11" x 4¾" x2 main piece
- 4¾" x 3¾" x2 top edge rectangle
- Trace two flap shapes from the template pattern piece and cut out.

5 Iron the Vilene Heavy Backing pieces in place as shown above, to the back of the two mailbox main pieces.

6 Cut two lengths of thin elastic approx. 3" (8cm) Fold them in half and pin them in place as marked in below.

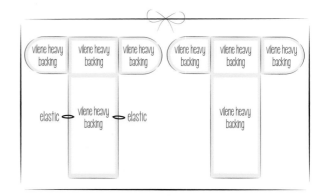

7 With wrong sides facing, place the two mailbox main pieces together, and machine top stitch all the way around the outer edge, making sure to catch the ends of the elastic between the layers.

8 Stitch two vintage/novelty buttons in place at the top of each flap.

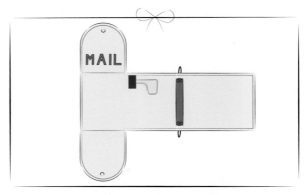

9 Fold the rectangle of the mailbox over and hand stitch the side in place. Close the flaps with the buttons.

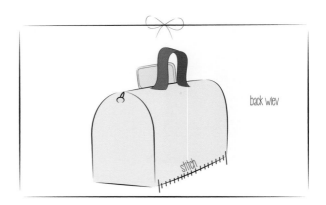

back view
stitch

Picking Parsnips!

*What a handy little satchel you have dear
Thistle, perfect for the parsnip harvest*

thistle

Thistle measures: 26cm (10") tall

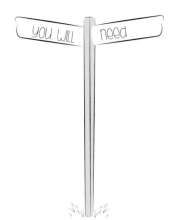
you will need

THISTLE

TEMPLATES ON PAGES 123-126

- 50cm x 40cm (20"x 16") light grey wool felt for rabbit head, body, ears, arms and legs
- 25cm x 20cm (10"x 8") ecru wool felt for tail, ears and parsnip
- 10cm x 5cm (4"x 2") leaf green wool felt for parsnip leaf
- 50cm x 40cm (20"x 16") fabric for dress
- 38cm x 30cm (15"x 12") linen for coat
- 23cm x 10cm (9"x 4") fabric for coat collar
- 30cm x 28cm (12"x 11") linen for satchel and strap
- 23cm x 18cm (9"x 7") fabric for satchel
- x2 6mm English glass dolls eyes
- Gutermann Upholstery thread for attaching the eyes
- Long doll making needle
- Sewing machine thread to match the felt
- Black embroidery thread
- x1 vintage /novelty button for coat
- x1 vintage /novelty button for satchel
- Jamieson's Shetland Spindrift 4ply yarn colour – Heron 315
- 2.75mm knitting needles for hand cuffs
- x2 white pipe cleaners for ears
- I" bias tape maker
- Toy fill
- General sewing supplies

A very tiny seam allowance is needed and included for Thistle, 3mm on all pieces.
A scant 1/4" seam allowance is used for the dress and coat and is also included

HEAD

* Head Gusset Diagrams are on page 12

1 Machine stitch around the head pieces leaving open where indicated at the base of the head. Leave the dart at the back of the head open at this stage. (see fig A)

2 Position the dart at the back of the head so that the seams match, machine stitch the dart from edge to edge, turn right side out, making sure to gently ease out all the curves. Stuff the head until very firm with toy fill. (see fig B)

3 Mark the position for the eyes with pins. Attach the English glass eyes per instructions on page 11 using Gutermann Upholstery Thread to match the felt. Anchor your thread inside the stuffing in the head opening.

4 Using 2 strand of black embroidery thread, stitch two back stitches either side of the pointed nose and two shorter back stitches underneath the first two, to form the mouth.

BODY

* Body Gusset Diagrams are on page 12

1 Use the same body as Mr. Oak. Machine stitch all the way around the body pieces leaving open where indicated at the back, leave the dart at the base of the body open at this stage. (see fig A)

2 Position the dart at the base of the body so that the seams come together, machine stitch the dart from edge to edge, turn right side out through the opening in the back, making sure to gently ease out all the curves and points. Stuff the body until very firm with toy fill. (see fig B)

3 Make a little hollow in the stuffing in the head and push the top of the body inside the head opening quite firmly, making sure the neat seam on the front of the body lines up with the front of the head. Place pins in to hold tight while you stitch the head on to the body, stuff a little more as you stitch if needed so the head is firmly attached.

LEGS

* Stitching/Attaching Leg Diagrams are on page 12

1 Cut out four legs from matching felt. Place two legs together and stitch all the way around the leg and foot leaving open where indicated at the back of the leg. Turn right side out and stuff the whole leg well. Hand stitch the leg closed tucking in the raw edge as you stitch. Repeat with the remaining leg.

2 Pin the legs in place on each side of the body, and with two strands of matching thread and a long doll making needle, stitch right through one leg through the body and out the other side of the other leg, keep going through in this fashion many times until the legs are firm, fasten off.

ARMS

* Stitching/Attaching Arm Diagrams are on page 12

1 Stitch the arms all the way around, leaving open where indicated, turn right side out and stuff the arms firmly, close the openings on the arms. Pin the arms to each side of the body just under the head and with two strands of matching thread and a long doll making needle, stitch right through one arm through the body and out the other side of the other arm, keep going through in this fashion many times until the arms are firm, fasten off.

EARS

1 Cut two ears from cream felt and two from the same colour felt as the body. Place them together in pairs each pair having one cream and one body colour. Machine stitch all the way around each ear leaving open where indicated, turn right side out, leaving the bottom straight edge open.

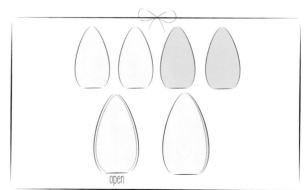

open

2 Cut approx. 23cm (9") length of pipe cleaner and fold it in half, gently mould the long sides of the pipe cleaner so they take on a slightly bowed 'V' shape.

3 Slide the pipe cleaner inside the ear and line up the pipe cleaner with the sides of the ear. Tuck under the raw open edge of the ear and stitch closed. Make a little fold in the straight end of each ear and hold with a small stitch.

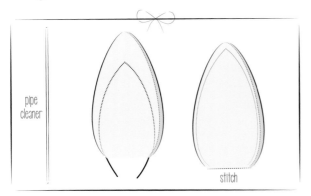

4 Pin the ears to the top of the head. Slightly curve the ears as you stitch them in place. The pipe cleaner will now allow you to mold the ears so they stay forward.

TAIL

1 Using matching thread to the felt gather by hand around the outer edge of the tail circle. Pull up the gathers so there is a small opening and fasten off but do not cut the thread yet. Stuff the tail until quite firm. Now stitch around the gathered circle again and pull the gathering until the opening is closed a little further. Stitch the tail to the back of the body.

DRESS

1 With right sides together, stitch two of the dress bodices all the way around, leaving open where indicated at the bottom straight edge.

2 Clip the corners and curves, turn right side out and press. Press under a tiny neat hem on the open straight edge.

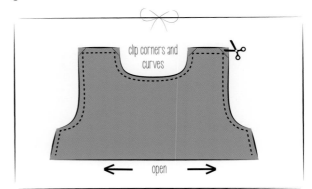

3 Cut 2 pieces of fabric for the skirt of the dress that measure 10" x 10" (25½cm x 25½cm). With right sides together, fold one of the skirt pieces in half and stitch down two sides, leaving open one long side. Clip corners, turn right side out and press.

4 Gather along the open, raw edge of the skirt through both thicknesses. Slide the gathered, raw edge of the skirt inside the open edge of the bodice. Adjust the gathers in the skirt to fit and hand stitch the skirt to the bodice.

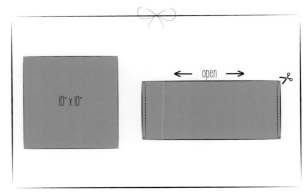

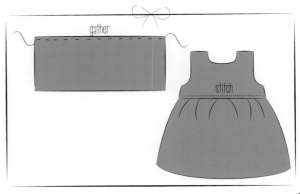

5 Repeat steps 1 - 4 for the remaining pieces.

6 You now have two identical dress pieces. Start to bring the two pieces together by hand stitching the shoulder seams and down the side seam on one side of the dress only.

7 Slide the dress over the rabbit's head and arm and now stitch the remaining shoulder seam and side seams.

COAT

1 With right sides together, place one coat bodice front on top of the coat bodice back matching shoulder seams, stitch the shoulder seam. Repeat with remaining front and shoulder seam.

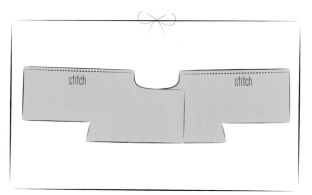

2 Open the piece out flat and press a neat seam in on both cuff edges on each sleeve and stitch in place.

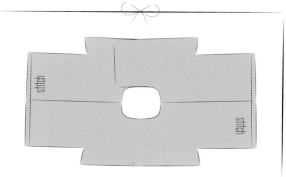

3 With right sides together, stitch along the under side of the sleeve seam and down the side seam, repeat on the other side. Make a tiny snip where the sleeve and the side seam meet.

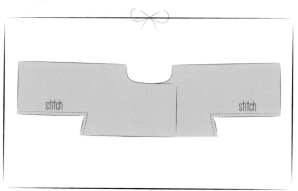

4 Cut a piece of matching linen for the coat bottom that measures 5" x 13" (13cm x 33cm). Fold the piece in half to find the centre and make a small pleat that measures approx. 1" (2cm). Add a few stitches to hold the pleat in place.

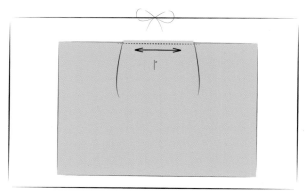

5 With right sides together, pin the coat bottom to the raw edge of the coat bodice, making sure that the pleat in the coat bottom is approx. in the centre back of the coat bodice. Machine stitch in place and press.

6 Press a neat hem in on the coat front and stitch in place. Turn up a neat hem on the coat bottom and stitch in place.

POCKET

1 With right sides together, stitch the two pocket pieces all the way around the outer edge, leaving open where indicated at the top. Clip the corners and the curves, turn right side out and press. Hand stitch the opening closed.

2 Machine stitch the pocket to on side of the coat front just around the curved edge.

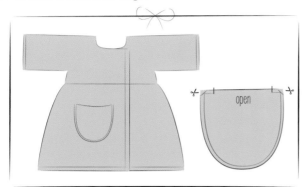

COAT COLLAR

1 With right sides together, stitch around the curved edge of the collar. Clip the curves, turn right side out and press. Press inside a tiny neat hem on the straight edge of the collar.

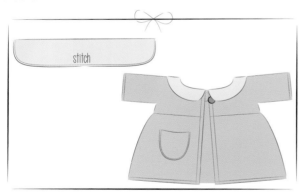

2 Slip the collar over the raw edge of the top of the coat bodice and hand stitch the collar in place. Fold the collar down and finger press. Stitch a vintage/novelty button in place to one side of the front of the bodice and make a small cotton loop to fasten. Place the coat on to Thistle and fasten the button.

KNITTED HAND CUFFS

* I used Jamieson's Shetland Spindrift 4 ply yarn colour: Heron 315

Cast on 30 stitches

1 Knit 1, purl 1 rib 4 rows.

2 Beginning with a knit row, stocking stitch 12 rows.

3 knit 1, purl 1 rib 4 rows

Cast off

4 Stitch the row ends of the hand cuff together. Weave the ends of the yarn in.

5 Repeat steps 1- 4 to make the second hand cuff. Place each hand cuff over the end of the arms over the sleeves of the coat.

SATCHEL

1 With right sides together, stitch all the way around the satchel, leaving open where indicated at one end.

2 Clip the corners and curves and turn the piece right side out and press. Hand stitch the opening closed.

3 Bring together one side with one rectangle end and hand stitch them together, repeat until all four sides are stitched.)

4 Using a 1" bias tape maker, make the following for the satchel strap:
x1 piece that measures: - 1½"x 12" (4cm x 30cm) long.
(see back pack diagrams for Mr. Oak

5 Tuck in the raw ends and top stitch the strap. Hand stitch the ends of the strap to either side of the satchel. Stitch a vintage/novelty button the one side of the satchel and hang the satchel over thistles shoulder.

PARSNIP

1 Cut one parsnip piece from ecru felt, bring the two straight sides of the parsnip piece together, and machine stitch, leaving open at the top of the parsnip.

2 Trim the tiny point off at the end of the parsnip, making sure not to cut the stitching, using a matching thread to the felt, hand gather around the top and quite close to the open edge.

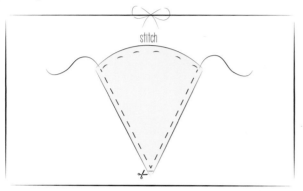

3 Turn the parsnip right side out, making sure to push the point out as far as it will go, Stuff the parsnip firmly.

4 Place the two parsnip leaves together and top stitch as shown.

5 Slide the end of the leaf inside the parsnip and pull up the gathers in the parsnip and fasten off making sure to catch the end of the leaf in the stitching.

6 Thread a long needle with 4 strands of cream embroidery thread. Make a knot in the end of the thread leaving a 'tail' approx 2cm (3/4"). Starting at the point of the parsnip, push the needle in and pull the thread until it stops at the knot, bring the needle out at the top of the parsnip and fasten off.

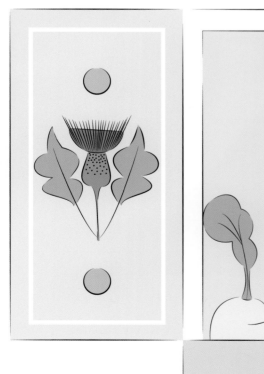

Hop Hop, Step and Hop!

gather and hide, tiny acorns.....

Sweet little twig warm in her pretty cape, gathering acorns in her homemade basket.

twig

Twig measures: 15cm (6") tall - Stepping Stone Mini Quilt measures: 18cm x 18cm (7 x 7")
Knitted Basket measures: 5cm (2") diameter

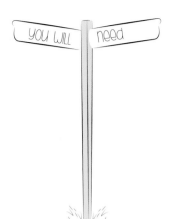
you will need

- 🍎 30cm x 23cm (12"x 9") chestnut red wool felt for squirrel head, ears, body, tail and arms
- 🍎 10cm x 7cm (4"x 3") light grey wool felt for inner ears
- 🍎 20cm x 18cm (8"x 7") aqua wool felt for cape
- 🍎 20cm x 18cm (8"x 7") fabric for cape
- 🍎 38cm x 5cm (15"x 2") white wool felt for cravat
- 🍎 24cm (9½") thin ribbon for cape
- 🍎 40cm x 20cm (16"x 8") neutral linen for mini quilt
- 🍎 28cm x 8cm (11"x 3") cream wool felt for tail tip and ears
- 🍎 20cm x 20cm (8"x 8") iron on batting for mini quilt
- 🍎 x9 different fabrics for stepping stone circles for mini quilt (2½"x 2½")
- 🍎 25cm x 25cm (10"x 10") thin iron on interfacing for mini quilt
- 🍎 82cm (32") 1" wide bias tape for mini quilt binding
- 🍎 x3 small neutral pom poms for acorns
- 🍎 Small scrap of thick cardboard for basket
- 🍎 Small scrap of fabric for basket base
- 🍎 2.75mm knitting needles

- 🍎 Jamieson's Shetland Spindrift 4ply yarn colour in Dog Rose - 268 and Moorit - 108
- 🍎 x2 4mm English glass dolls eyes
- 🍎 Gutermann Upholstery thread for attaching the eyes
- 🍎 Long doll making needle
- 🍎 Sewing machine thread to match the felt
- 🍎 Black embroidery thread
- 🍎 Toy fill
- 🍎 Craft glue
- 🍎 General sewing supplies

A very tiny seam allowance is needed and included for the twig, 3mm on all pieces

A scant 1/4" seam allowance is used for the her cape and stepping stone mini quilt and is also included.

HEAD

* Head Gusset Diagrams are on page 12

1 Machine stitch around the head pieces leaving open where indicated at the base of the head, leave the dart at the back of the head open at this stage. (see fig A)

2 Position the dart at the back of the head so that the seams match, machine stitch the dart from edge to edge, turn right side out, making sure to gently ease out all the curves and the point of the snout. Stuff the head and snout until very firm with toy fill. (see fig B)

FACE

1 Mark the position for the eyes with pins. Attach the English glass eyes per instructions on page 11 using Gutermann Upholstery Thread to match the felt. Anchor your thread inside the stuffing in the head opening.

2 Using two strands of black embroidery thread, stitch a few backstitches over each other on the tip of the nose. Pass the thread back through the stitches and stitch a small "V" at the base of the nose, fasten off. Stitch an eyelash on the outer side of each eye.

BODY

1 Machine stitch all the way around the body pieces leaving open where indicated at the side.

2 Turn the body right side out through the opening in the side, making sure to gently ease out the little legs. Stuff the body until firm with toy fill, close the opening.

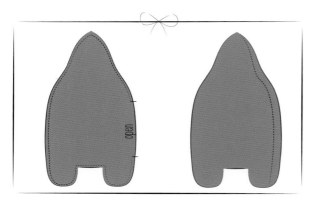

3 Make a little hollow in the stuffing in the head and push the top of the body inside the head opening quite firmly, place pins in to hold the head on tight while you stitch the head on to the body, stuff a little more as you stitch if needed so the head is firmly on the body.

ARMS

* Stitching/Attaching Arm Diagrams are on page 12

1 Stitch the arms all the way around, leaving open where indicated, turn right side out and stuff the arms firmly in the 'hands' and place less stuffing in the 'top' of the arm, close the openings on the arms.

2 Pin the arms to each side of the body just under the head and with two strands of Gutermann Upholstery Thread and a long doll making needle, stitch right through one arm through the body and out the other side of the other arm, keep going through in this fashion many times until the arms are firm, fasten off.

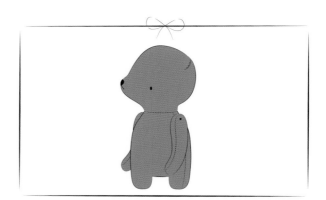

EARS

1 Cut two ears from light grey wool felt and two from the same colour as the head. Place them together in pairs each pair having one light grey one head colour ear.

2 Machine stitch all the way around each ear leaving open where indicated, turn right side out.

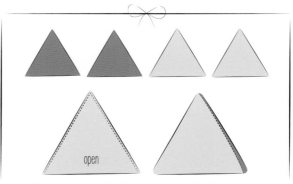

3 Make a little fold in the straight end of each ear and hold with a small stitch.

4 Pin the ears in place, making sure the folded front of each ear faces to the side of the head. Stitch the ears in place tucking in a small raw edge as you stitch.

TAIL

1 Machine stitch the two tail pieces all the way around leaving open where indicated. Clip curves and turn right side out. Stuff the tail very firmly and pin to the bottom of the body. Hand stitch the tail in position tucking in a tiny raw edge as you stitch.

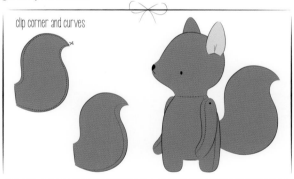

clip corner and curves

CAPE

1 With right sides together, make two tiny pleats in the curved upper edge of both the felt and fabric cape pieces. Stitch them in place as shown from the top curved edge, tapering them to a point as you stitch.

pleat   pleat

open

2 Cut two lengths of thin ribbon, approx. 12cm (5") long. Pin them in between the two layers as shown.

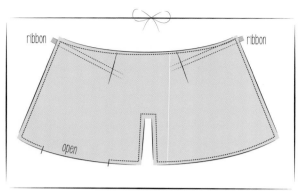

ribbon   ribbon

open

3 With right sides together, stitch the cape all the way around the outer edge, leaving open where indicated and making sure to catch the end of the ribbon in the stitching.

4 Clip the corners and turn the cape right side out and press. Hand stitch the opening closed. Tie the ends of the ribbon in a knot. Leave aside for now.

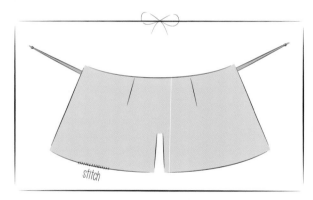

stitch

CAPE COLLAR

1 Using the stitch guide on page 10 stitch two tiny Daisy stitch leaves in green and one French knot flower in pink in each corner of the felt collar piece as shown.

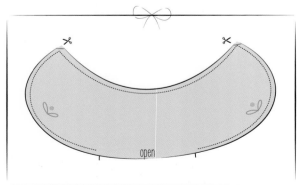

open

2 With right sides together, stitch all the way around the outer edge of the collar, leaving open where indicated.

3 Clip the corners, turn the collar right side out and press. Hand stitch the opening closed.

4 Pin the upper curved edge of the collar (with the felt side outermost) to the top curved edge of the cape and hand stitch it in place. Tie the cape around the squirrel's neck.

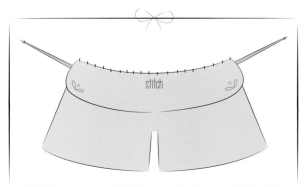

STEPPING STONE MINI QUILT

1 To make the mini quilt, cut the following:
x9 different fabrics for the stepping stones - 2½"x 2½" each
x2 pieces of linen for the background and backing - 8" x 8"
x1 piece of iron on batting - 8" x 8"

2 Cut the light weight iron on interfacing in to nine 2½"x 2½" squares.

3 Trace the stepping stone template on to the centre of each square of interfacing.

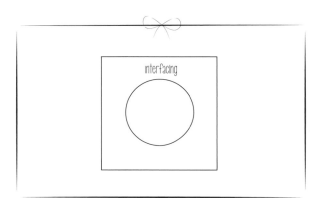

4 With the right side of the fabric facing the glue side of the interfacing, machine stitch around the circle you traced. Cut out the circles leaving a scant ¼" seam allowance.

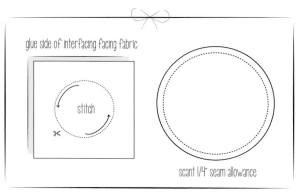

5 Pinch the interfacing away from the fabric and make a small slit in the interfacing and turn the circles right side out. Smoothing around the edge.

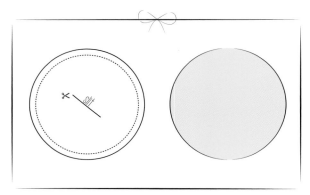

6 Place all the circles in a 3 x 3 grid in the centre of one of the pieces of linen. Iron them in place, hand stitch around each circle to secure them in place.

7 Iron the batting to the wrong side of the linen and place the remaining piece of linen wrong side facing the batting. Trim the mini quilt to measure 7"x 7".

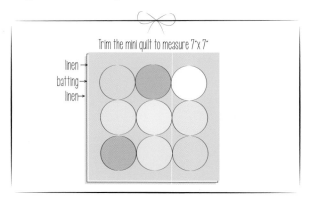

8   Bind the mini quilt with the bias tape, open out the tape and using the crease as a guide, stitch the tape to the front of the mini quilt, keeping raw edges even and mitring the corners. Fold the tape to the back and hand stitch in place.

KNITTED BASKET

* I used Jamieson's Shetland Spindrift 4 ply yarn in Dog Rose -268

1   Cast on 11 stitches.

2   Purl

3   Knit 2 (m1,k1) 8 times, k1 (19 stitches)

4   Purl

5   Knit 2 (m1,k1) 16 times, k1 (35 stitches)

6   Purl

7   Knit

8   Purl

9   Knit 3, m1, (k2, m1) 6 times, k3, m1 (k2,m1) 7 times, k3 (50 stitches)

10   Purl

11   Knit 1, p1 to the end

12   Purl 1, k1 to the end

13   Repeat rows 11 and 12 - x4 more times

14   Knit 1, p1 to the end

15   Join on an extra strand of yarn and purl one row with two strands.

16   Cast off knit wise with both strands.

17   Join row ends together, gather by hand around the small base. Pull up the gathers and fasten off. Weave in any remaining ends of yarn.

18   Cut a 4cm circle from sturdy cardboard and one slightly larger from fabric. Stick the circle of card to the wrong side of the fabric, in the centre. Cut slits all the way around the fabric and glue the tabs to the back of the cardboard. Glue the fabric circle inside the bottom of the basket.

KNITTED ACORN CAPS

* I used Jamieson's Shetland Spindrift 4 ply yarn in Moorit - 108

1   Cast on 20 stitches

2   Knit

3   Knit

4   Purl

5   Knit 1, knit 2 together (6 times) k2 - 14 stitches

6   Purl

7   Knit 2 together to the end - 7 stitches

8   Purl

9   Knit 2 together (3 times) k1 - 4 stitches

10   Cut the yarn from the ball leaving a long tail. Thread the yarn tail on to a large bodkin and thread it through the remaining 4 stitches on the knitting needle, pulling the knitting needle out. Pull up the stitches tightly and fasten off (don't cut the yarn yet). Stitch the row ends of the acorn cap together. Weave the ends of the yarn in.

11   Hand stitch the acorn cap to the top of the pom pom. Make three in total.

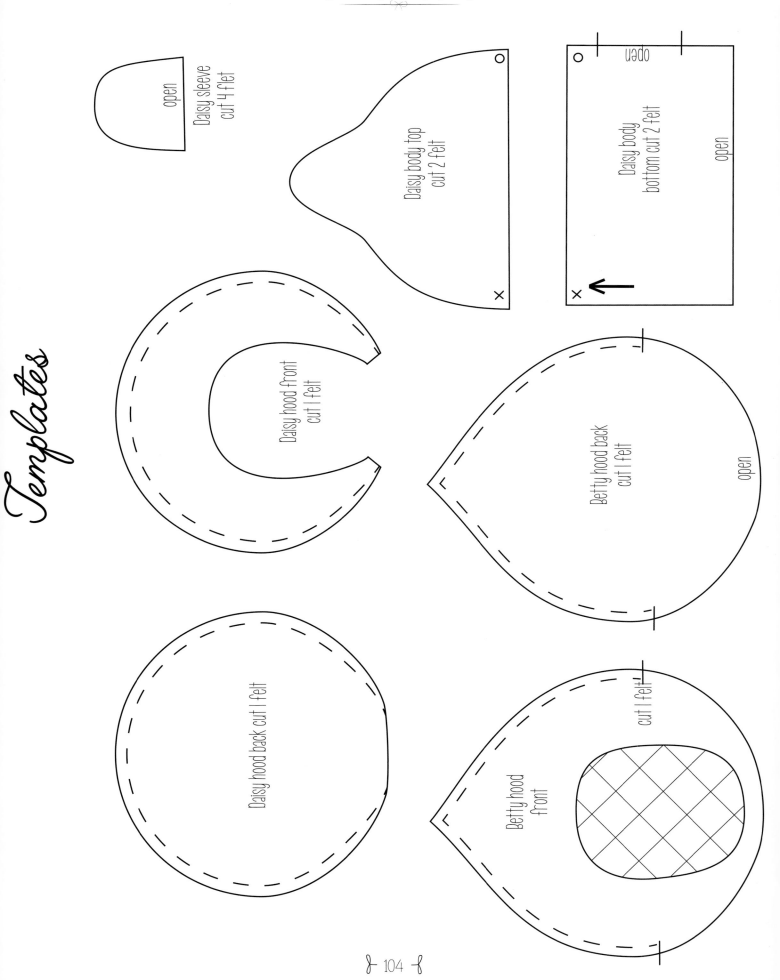

Templates

open

Daisy sleeve
cut 4 felt

Daisy body top
cut 2 felt

open

Daisy body
bottom cut 2 felt

open

Daisy hood front
cut 1 felt

Betty hood back
cut 1 felt

open

Daisy hood back cut 1 felt

Betty hood
front

cut 1 felt

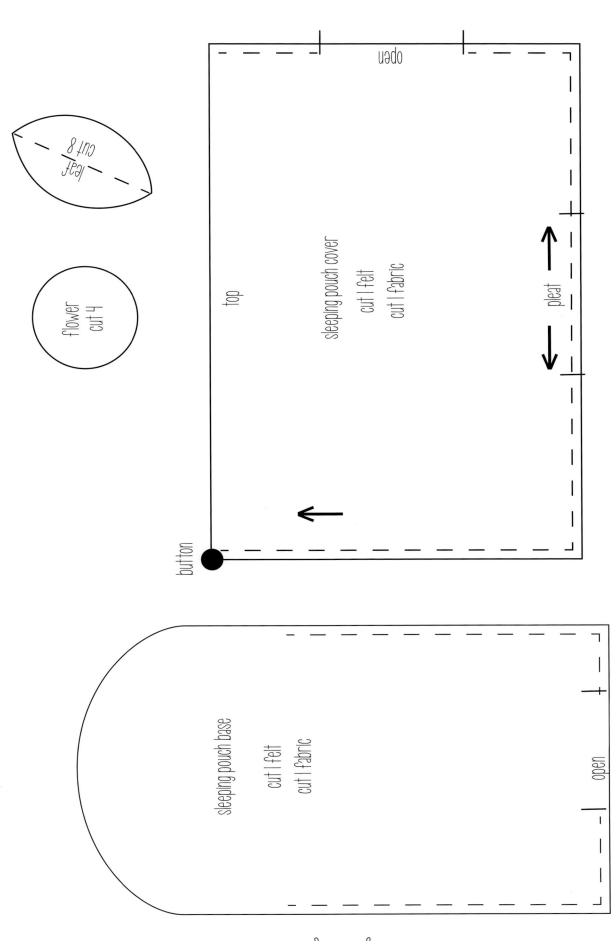

leaf
cut 8

flower
cut 4

open

top

sleeping pouch cover

cut 1 felt
cut 1 fabric

pleat

button

sleeping pouch base

cut 1 felt
cut 1 fabric

open

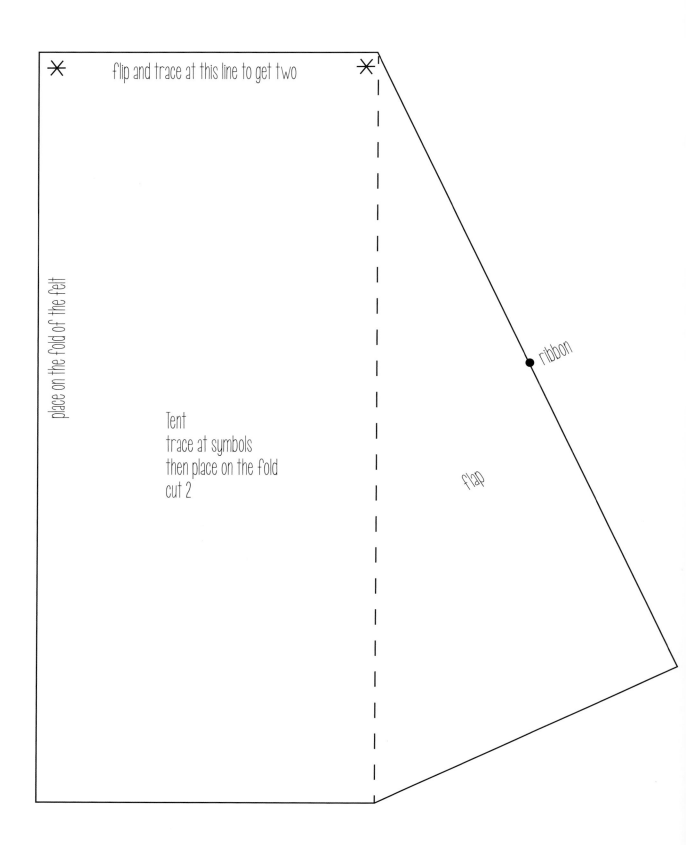

flip and trace at this line to get two

place on the fold of the felt

Tent
trace at symbols
then place on the fold
cut 2

ribbon

flap

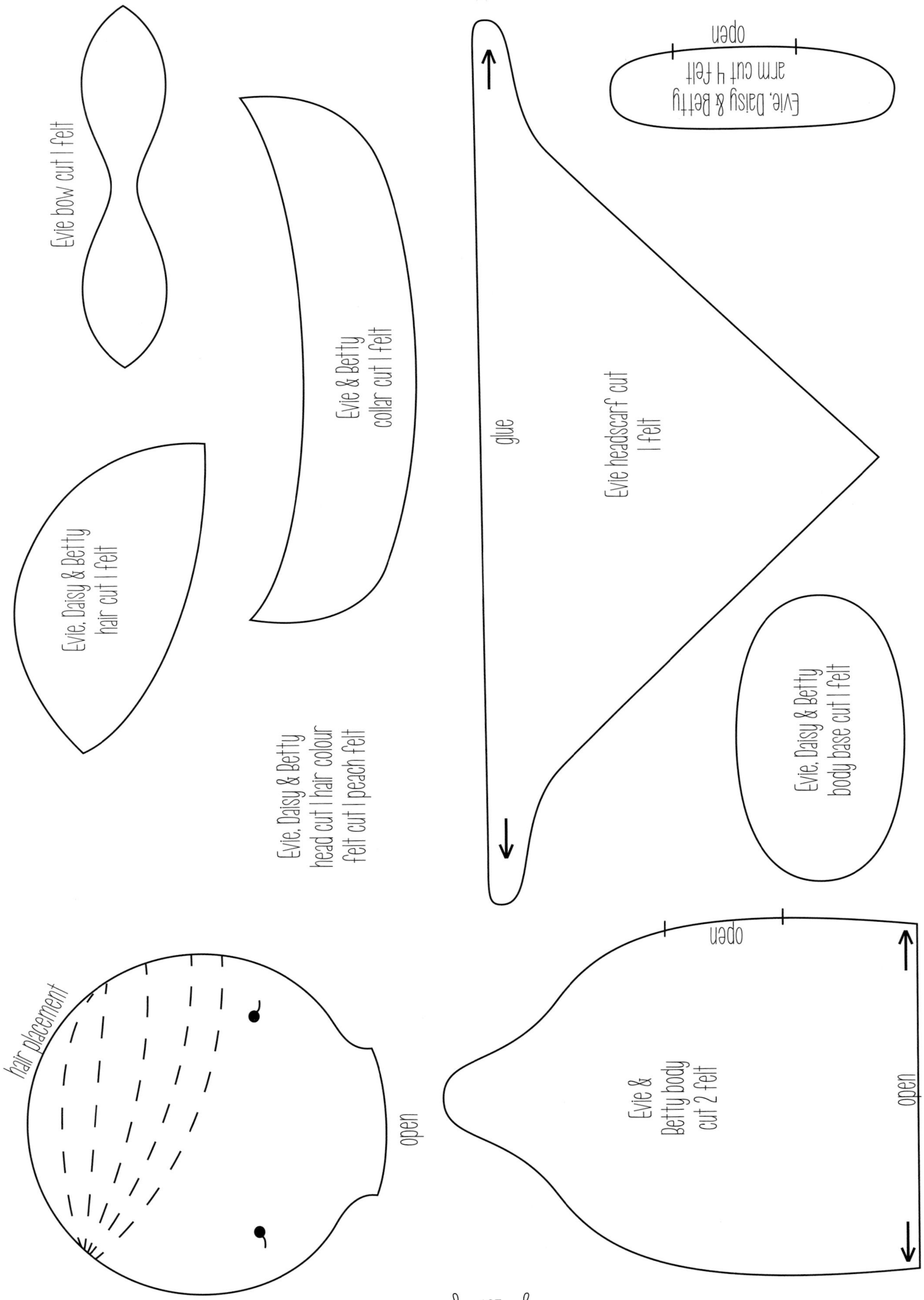

Evie bow cut 1 felt

Evie, Daisy & Betty
arm cut 4 felt

open

glue

Evie & Betty
collar cut 1 felt

Evie headscarf cut
1 felt

Evie, Daisy & Betty
hair cut 1 felt

Evie, Daisy & Betty
head cut 1 hair colour
felt cut 1 peach felt

Evie, Daisy & Betty
body base cut 1 felt

hair placement

open

open

Evie &
Betty body
cut 2 felt

open

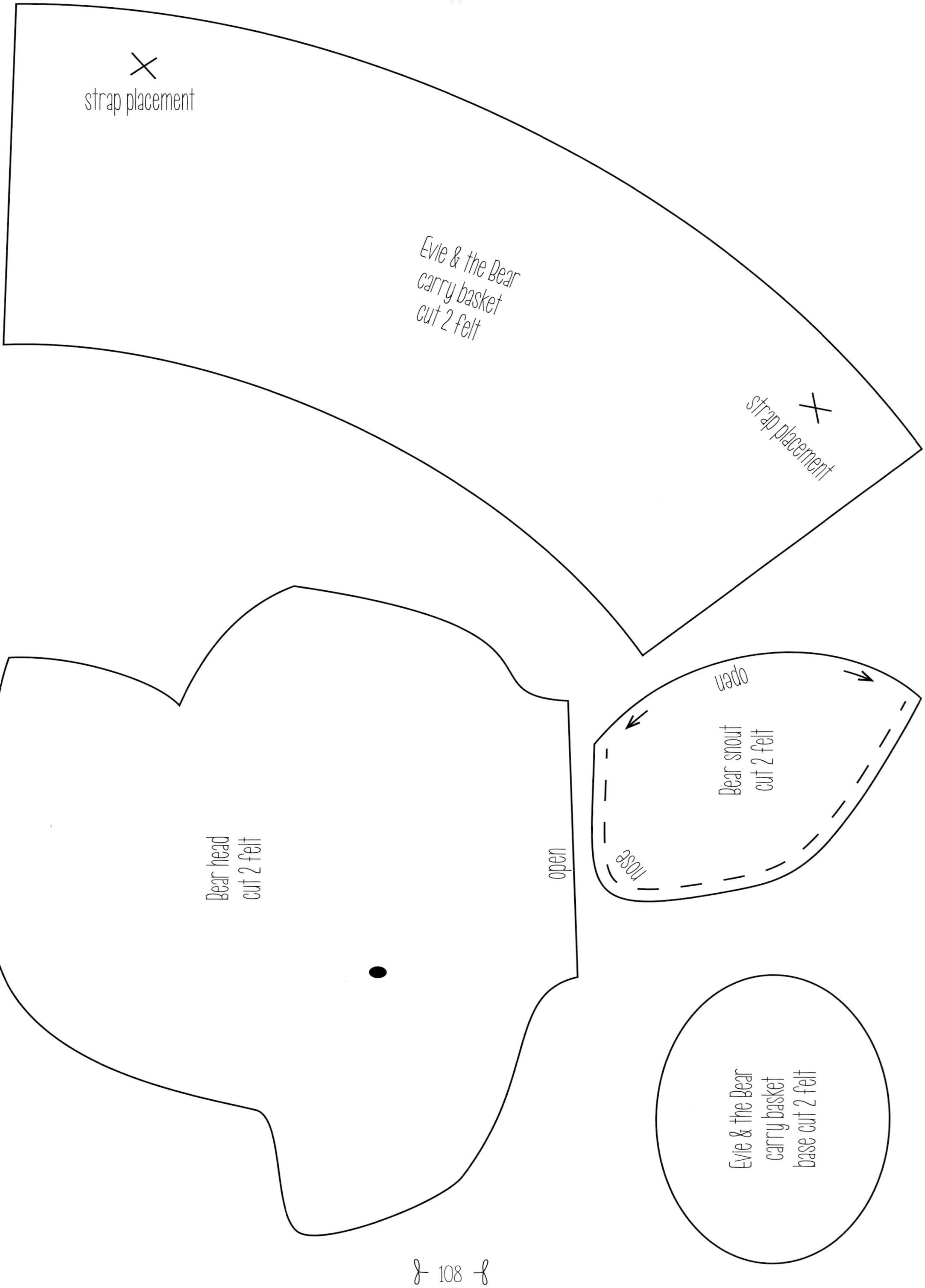

X
strap placement

Evie & the Bear
carry basket
cut 2 felt

strap placement
X

Bear head
cut 2 felt

open

Bear snout
cut 2 felt

open

nose

Evie & the Bear
carry basket
base cut 2 felt

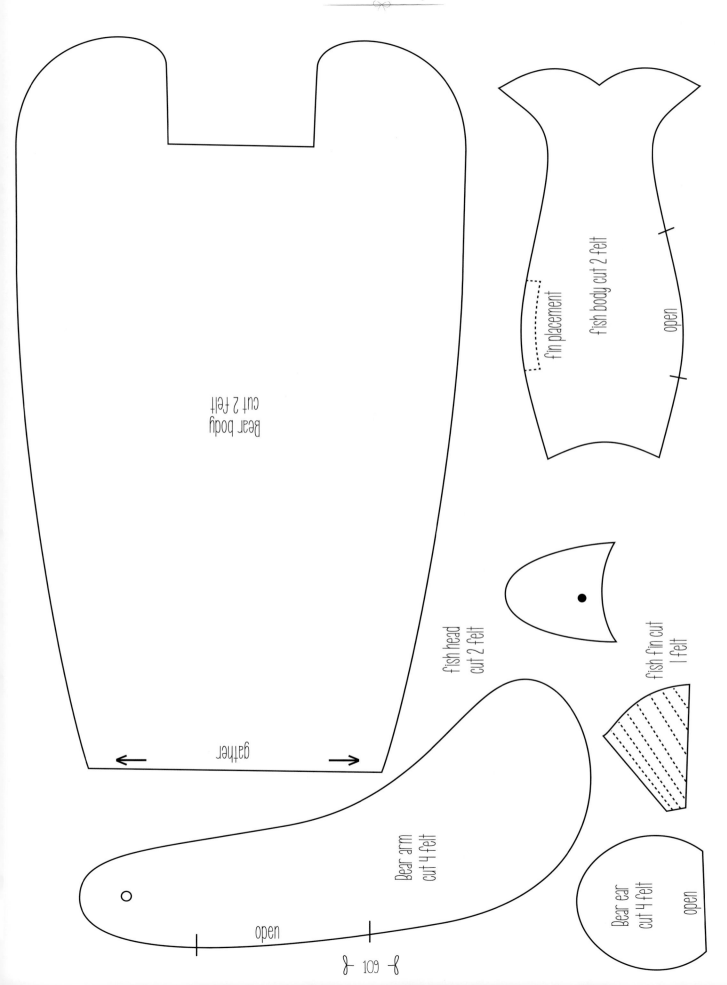

Bear body
cut 2 felt

fish body cut 2 felt

fin placement

open

fish head
cut 2 felt

fish fin cut
1 felt

gather

Bear arm
cut 4 felt

Bear ear
cut 4 felt

open

open

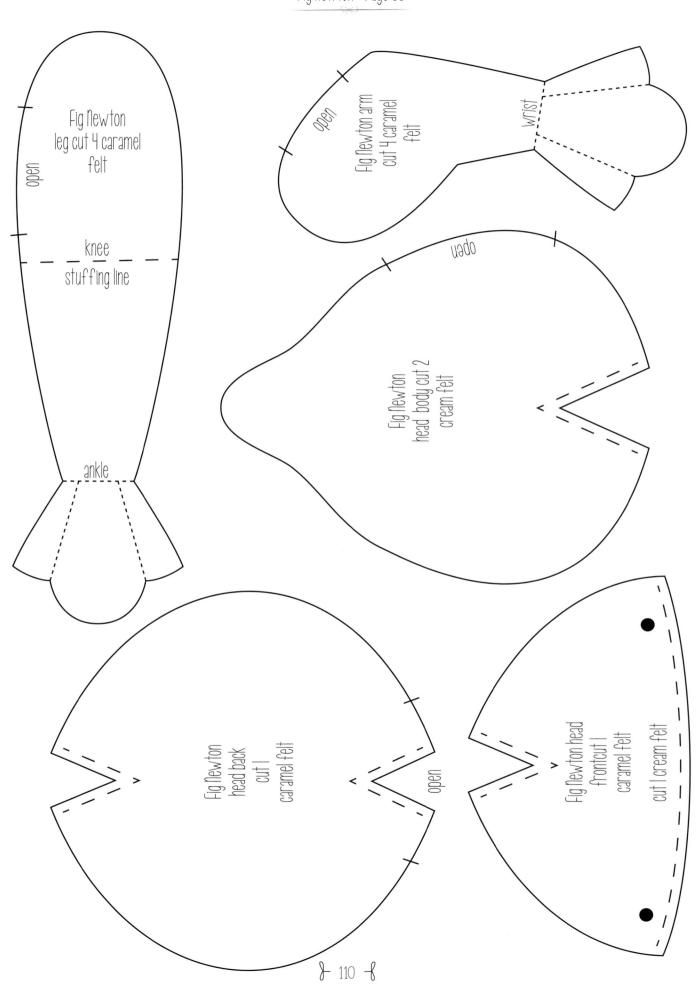

Fig Newton
leg cut 4 caramel
felt

open

knee
stuffing line

ankle

open

Fig Newton arm
cut 4 caramel
felt

wrist

open

Fig Newton
head body cut 2
cream felt

Fig Newton
head back
cut 1
caramel felt

open

Fig Newton head
front cut 1
caramel felt

cut 1 cream felt

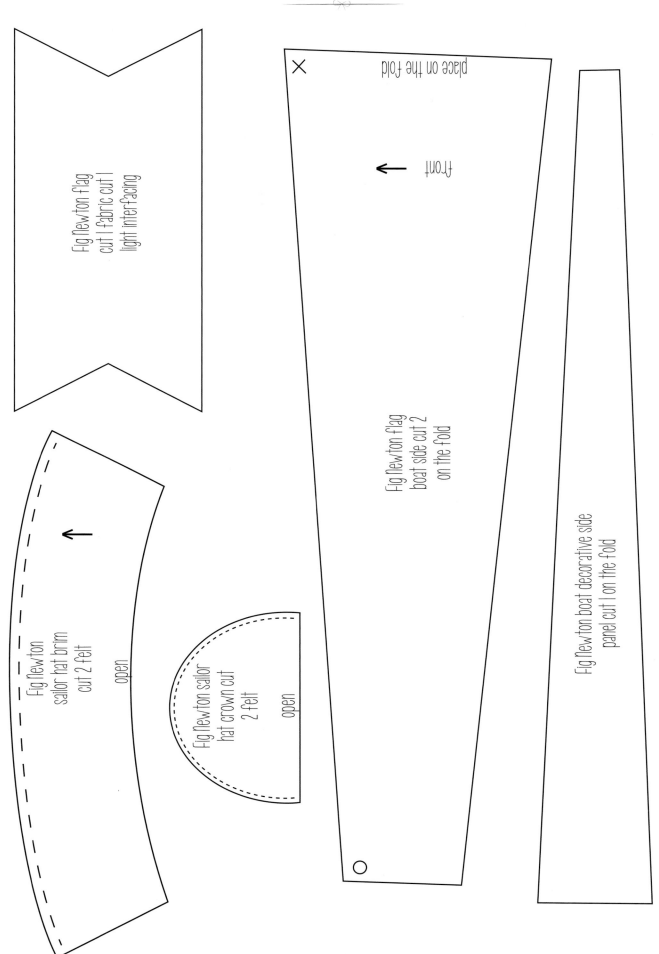

Fig Newton flag
cut 1 fabric cut 1
light interfacing

place on the fold

✕

front

Fig Newton flag
boat side cut 2
on the fold

Fig Newton
sailor hat brim
cut 2 felt

open

Fig Newton sailor
hat crown cut
2 felt

open

Fig Newton boat decorative side
panel cut 1 on the fold

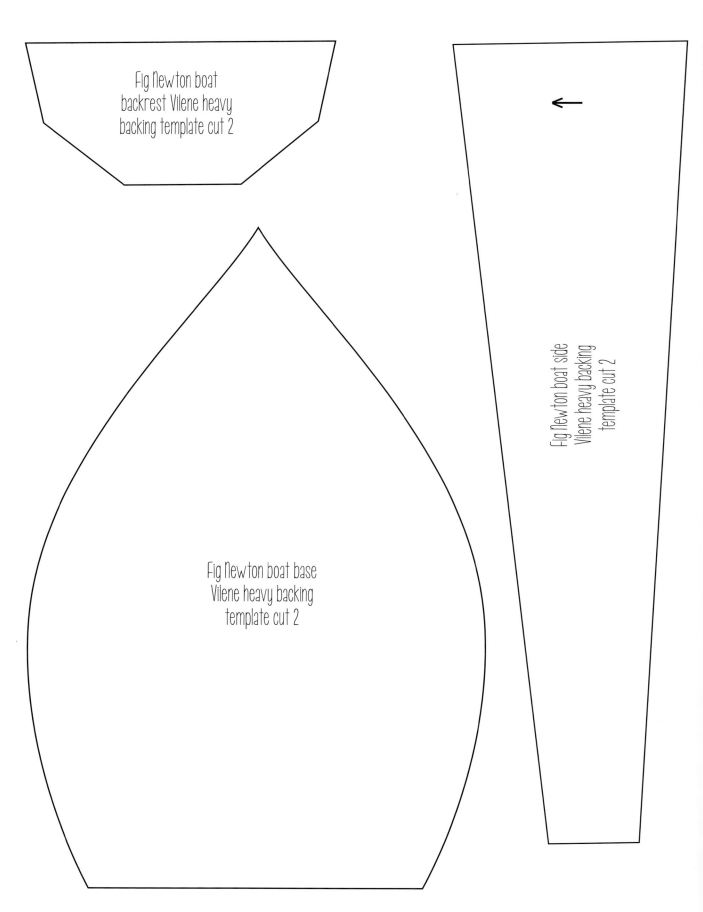

Fig Newton boat
backrest Vilene heavy
backing template cut 2

Fig Newton boat base
Vilene heavy backing
template cut 2

Fig Newton boat side
Vilene heavy backing
template cut 2

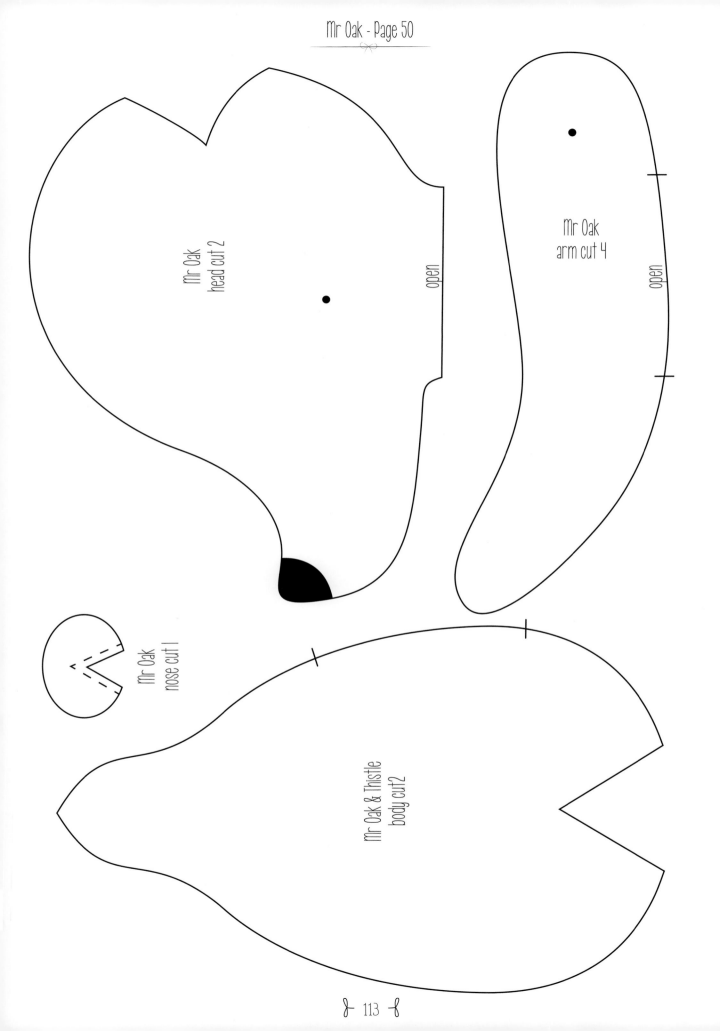

Mr Oak
head cut 2

open

Mr Oak
arm cut 4

open

Mr Oak
nose cut 1

Mr Oak & Thistle
body cut2

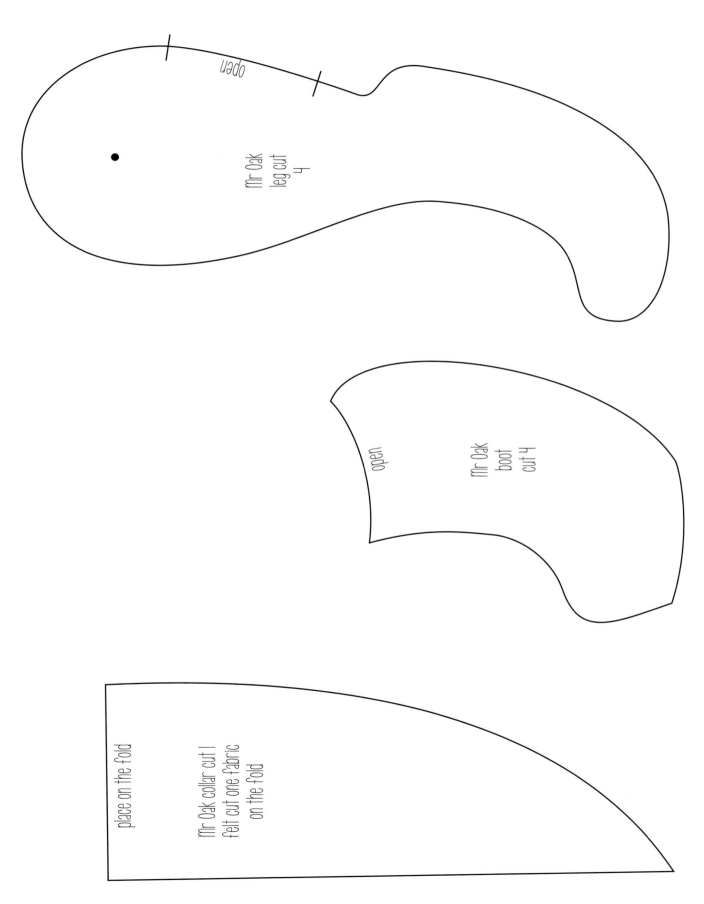

open

Mr Oak
leg cut
4

open

Mr Oak
boot
cut 4

place on the fold

Mr Oak collar cut 1
felt cut one fabric
on the fold

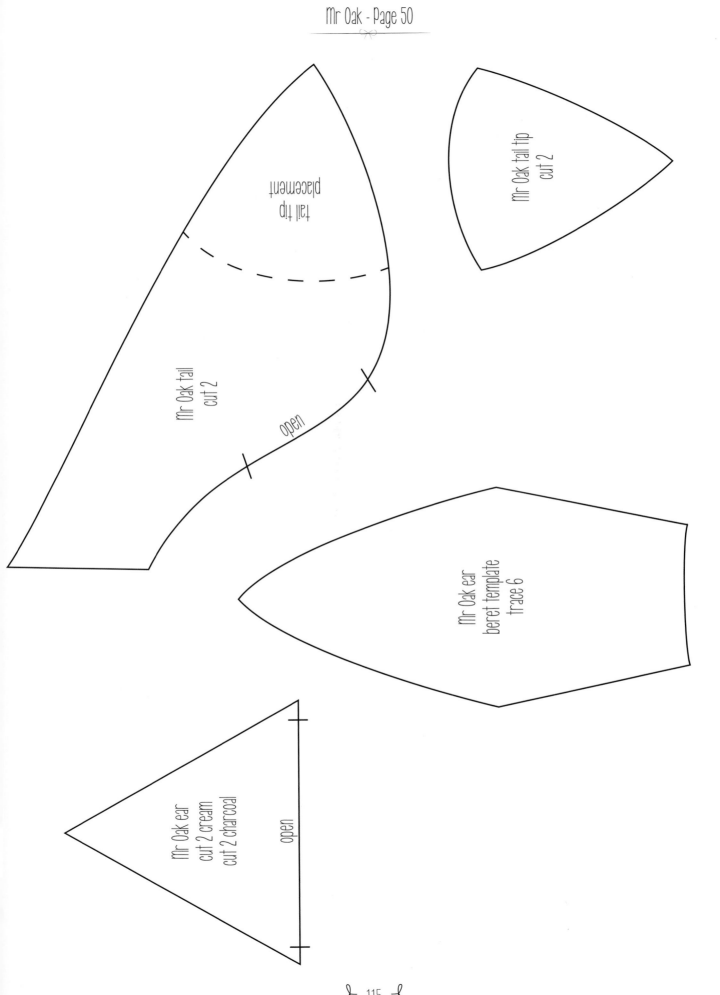

Mr Oak tail tip
cut 2

tail tip
placement

Mr Oak tail
cut 2

open

Mr Oak ear
beret template
trace 6

Mr Oak ear
cut 2 cream
cut 2 charcoal

open

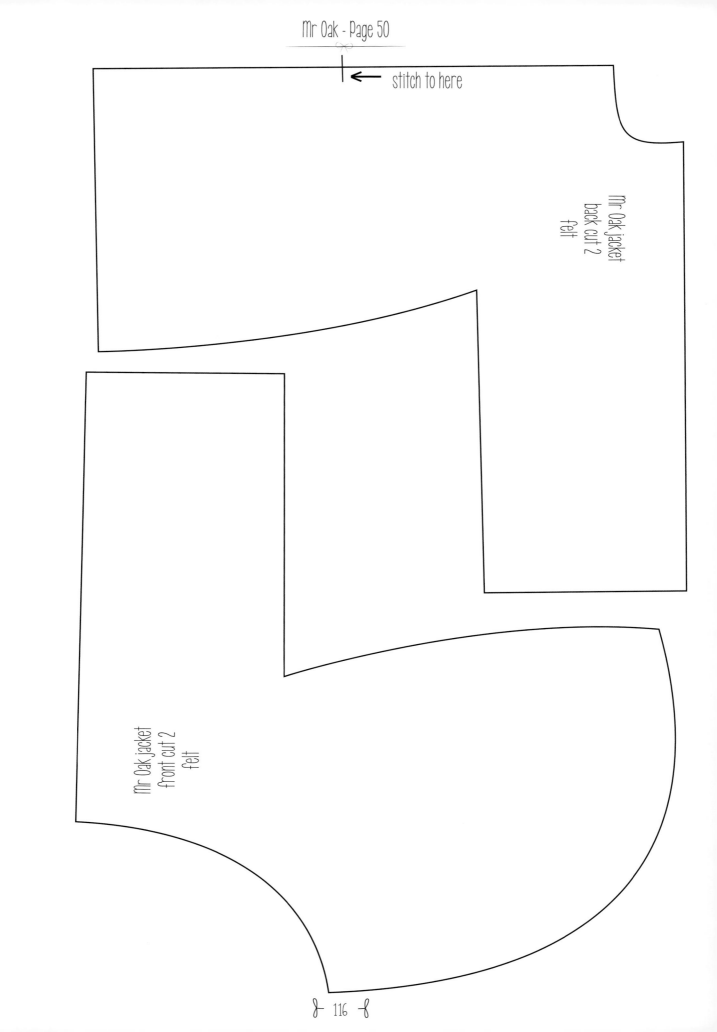

stitch to here

Mr Oak jacket
back cut 2
felt

Mr Oak jacket
front cut 2
felt

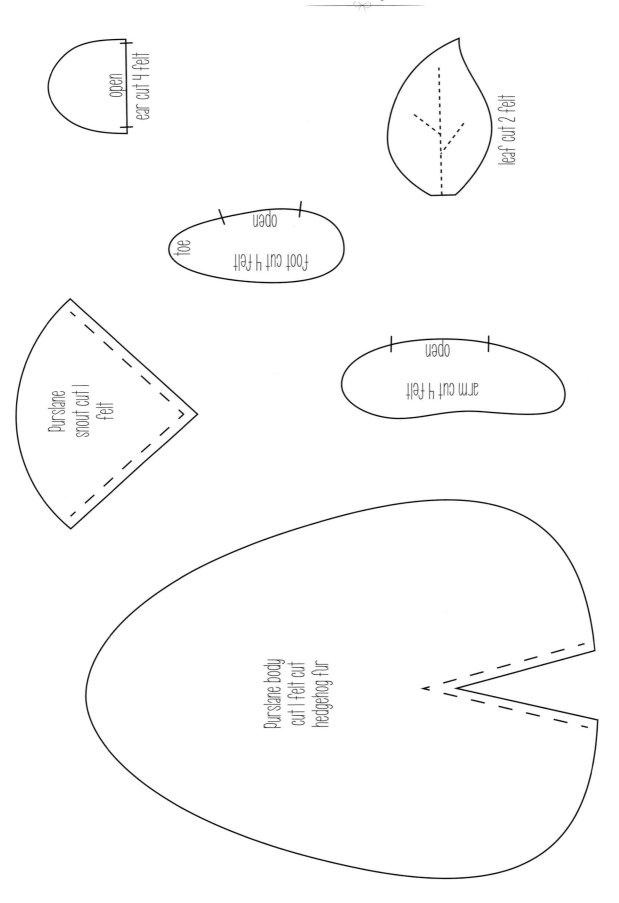

open
ear cut 4 felt

leaf cut 2 felt

toe
open
foot cut 4 felt

open
arm cut 4 felt

Purslane
snout cut 1
felt

Purslane body
cut 1 felt cut
hedgehog fur

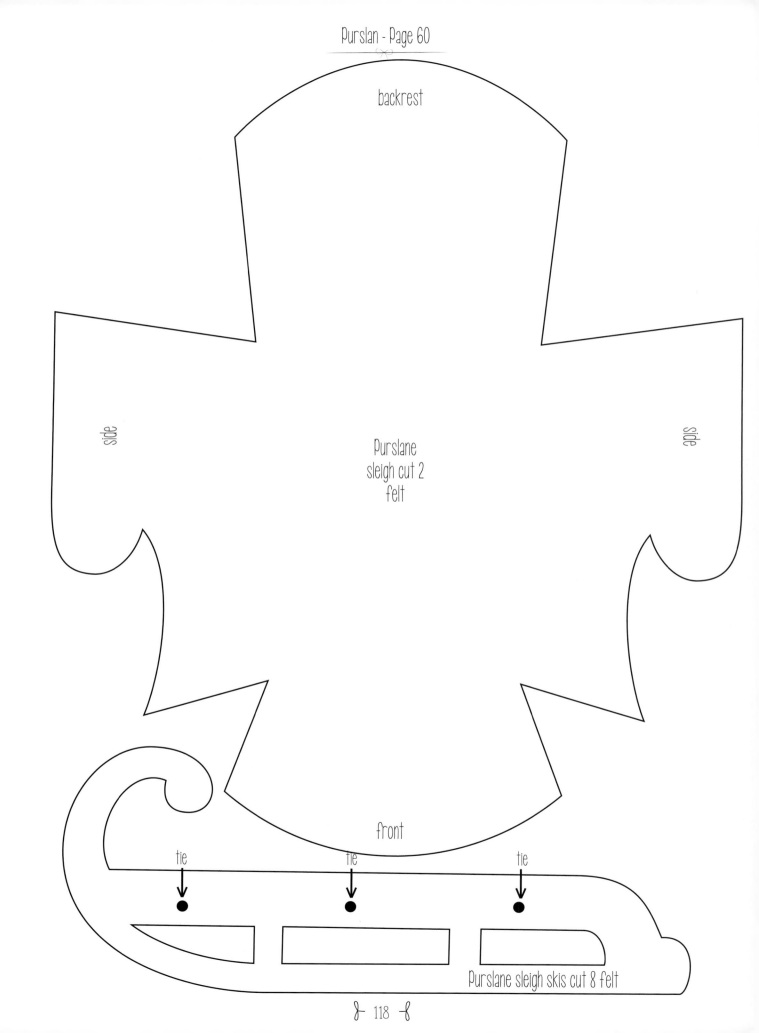

backrest

side

side

Purslane
sleigh cut 2
felt

front

tie

tie

tie

Purslane sleigh skis cut 8 felt

Purslane sleigh front Vilene heavy backing template cut 2

Purslane sleigh side Vilene heavy backing template cut 2 (x2 in reverse)

Purslane sleigh base Vilene heavy backing template cut 2

Purslane sleigh back Vilene heavy backing template cut 2

Purslane sleigh skis Vilene heavy backing template cut 8 (x4 in reverse)

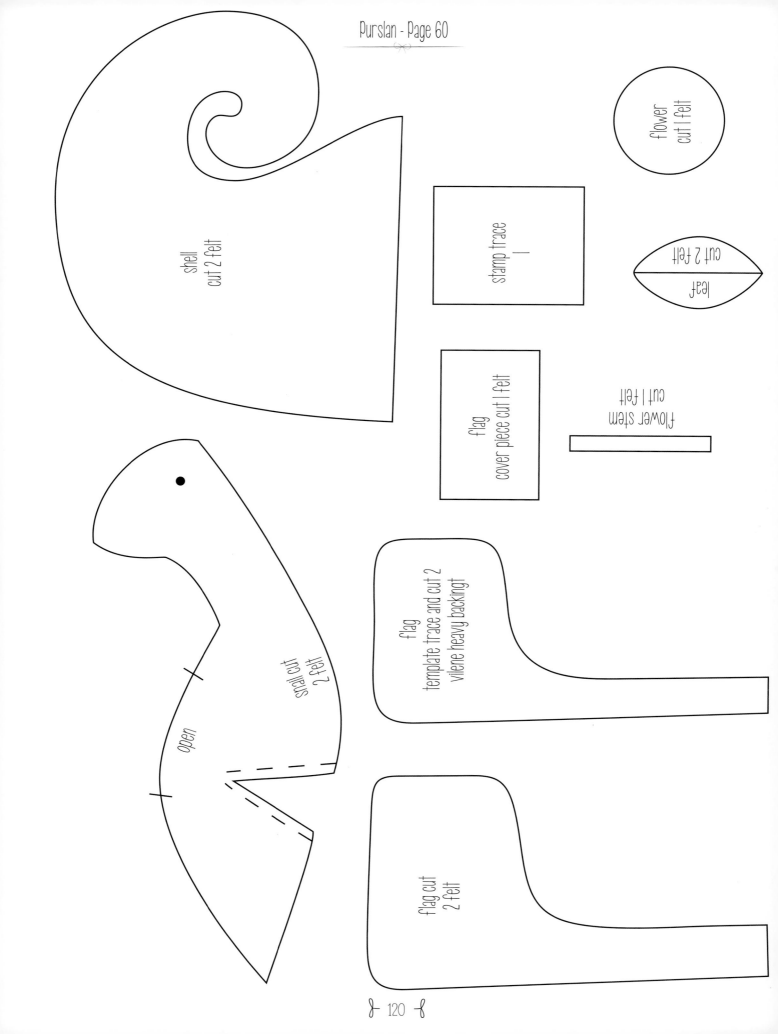

flower
cut 1 felt

shell
cut 2 felt

stamp trace
1

leaf
cut 2 felt

flag
cover piece cut 1 felt

flower stem
cut 1 felt

snail cut
2 felt

open

flag
template trace and cut 2
vilene heavy backingt

flag cut
2 felt

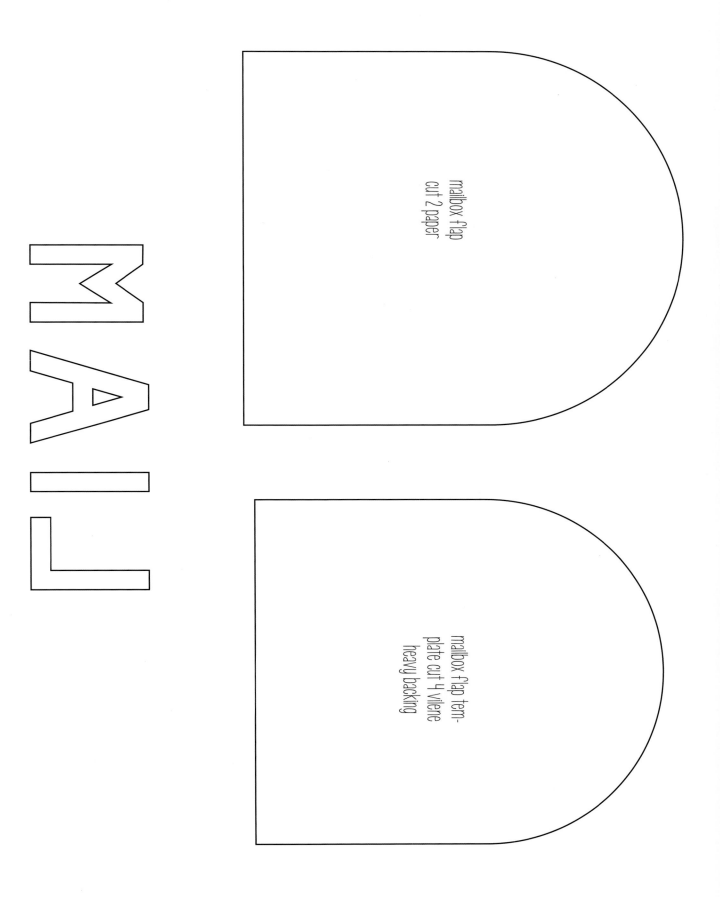

MAIL

mailbox flap
cut 2 paper

mailbox flap tem-
plate cut 4 vilene
heavy backing

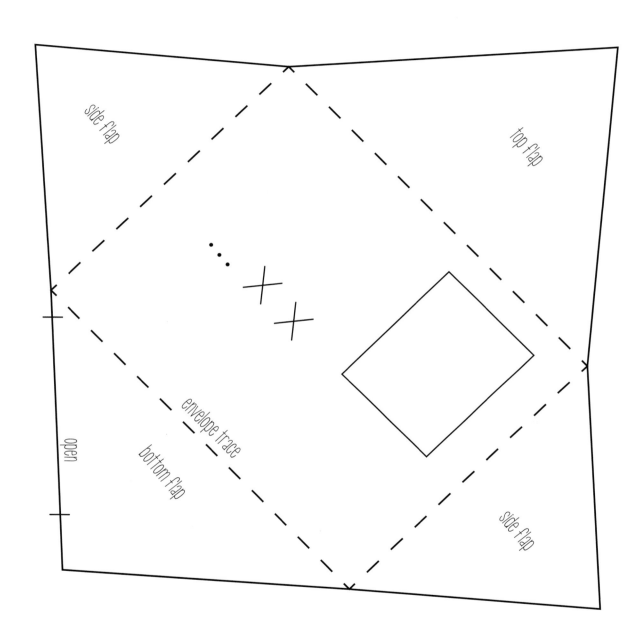

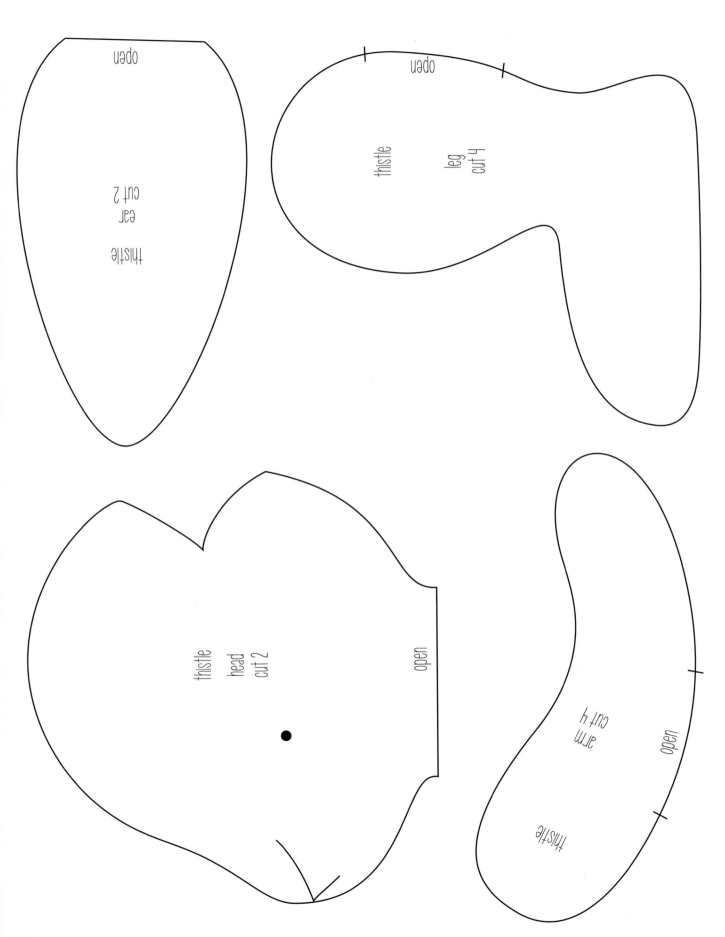

thistle
ear
cut 2

open

thistle
leg
cut 4

open

thistle
head
cut 2

open

thistle
arm
cut 4

open

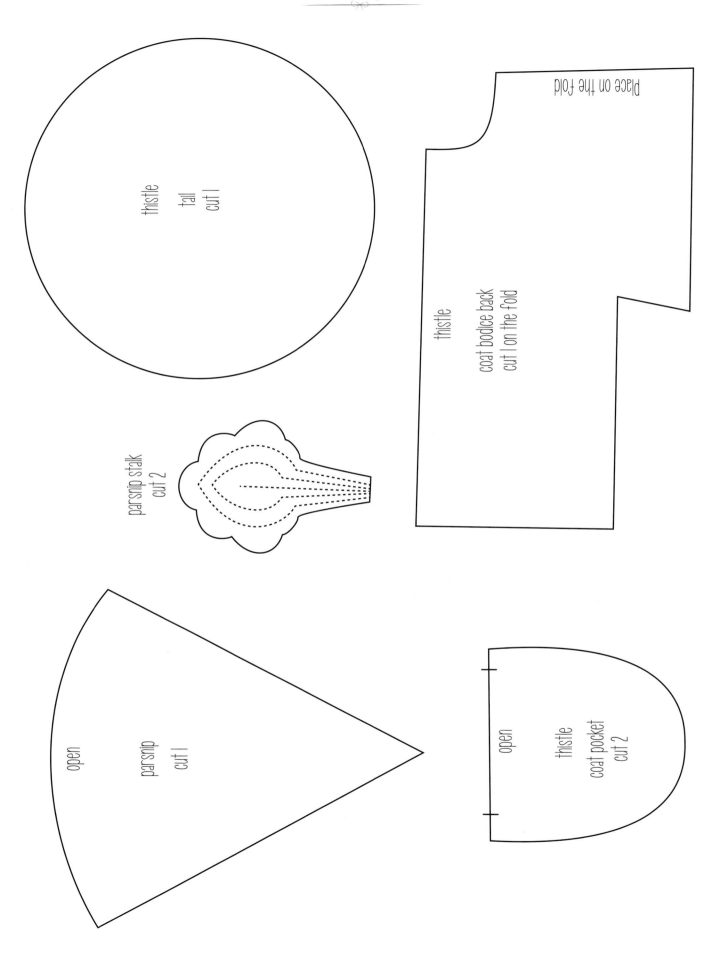

thistle
tail
cut 1

parsnip stalk
cut 2

thistle
coat bodice back
cut 1 on the fold

Place on the fold

open

parsnip
cut 1

open

thistle
coat pocket
cut 2

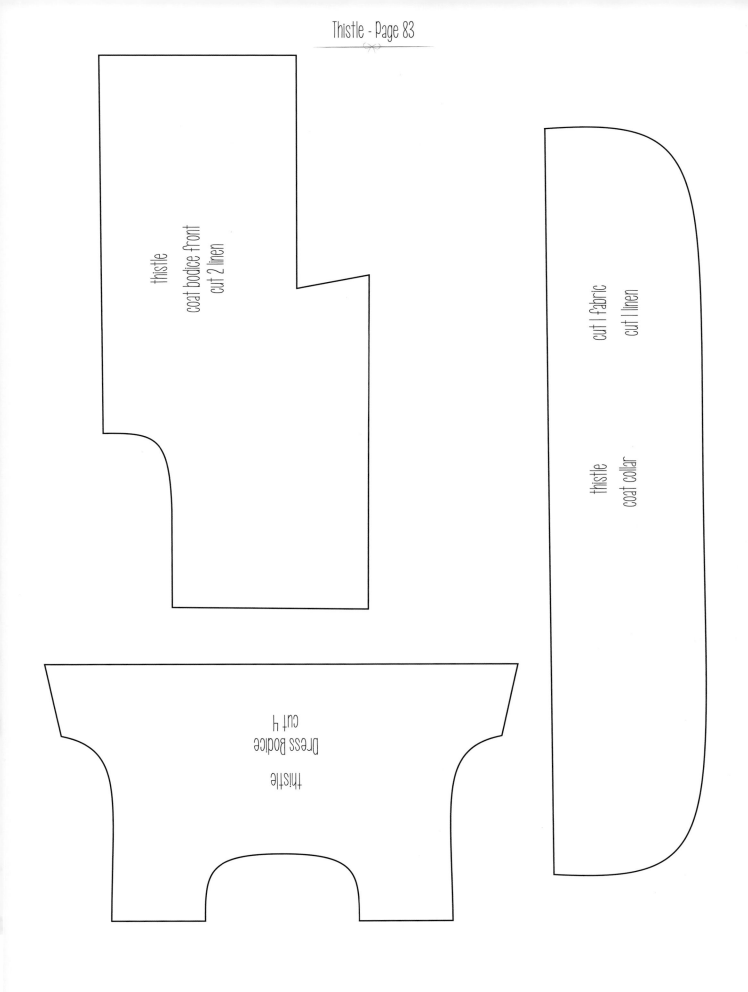

thistle
coat bodice front
cut 2 linen

cut 1 fabric
cut 1 linen

thistle
coat collar

thistle
Dress Bodice
cut 4

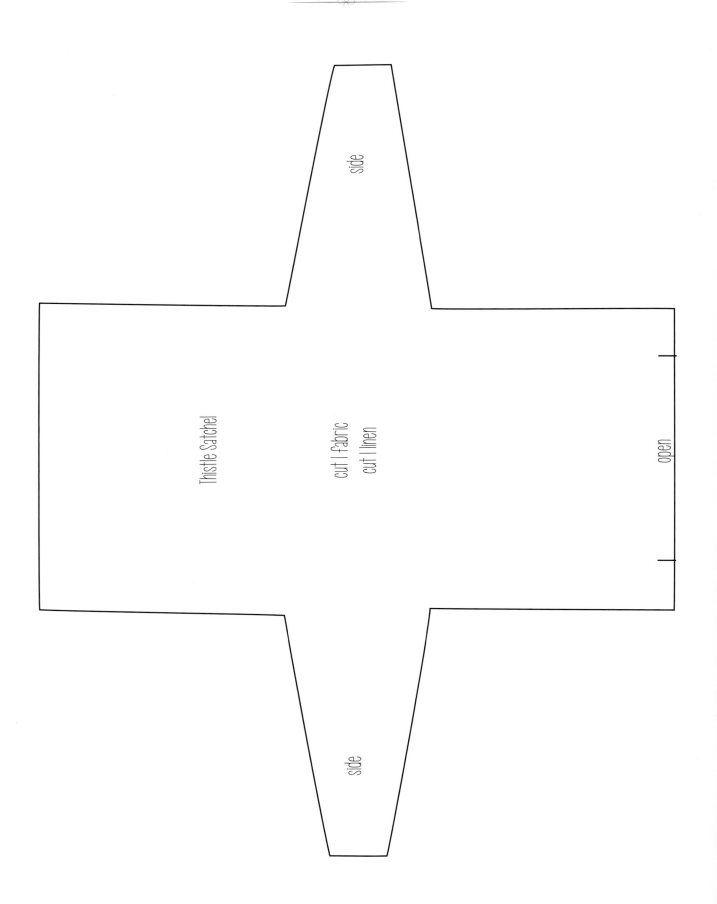

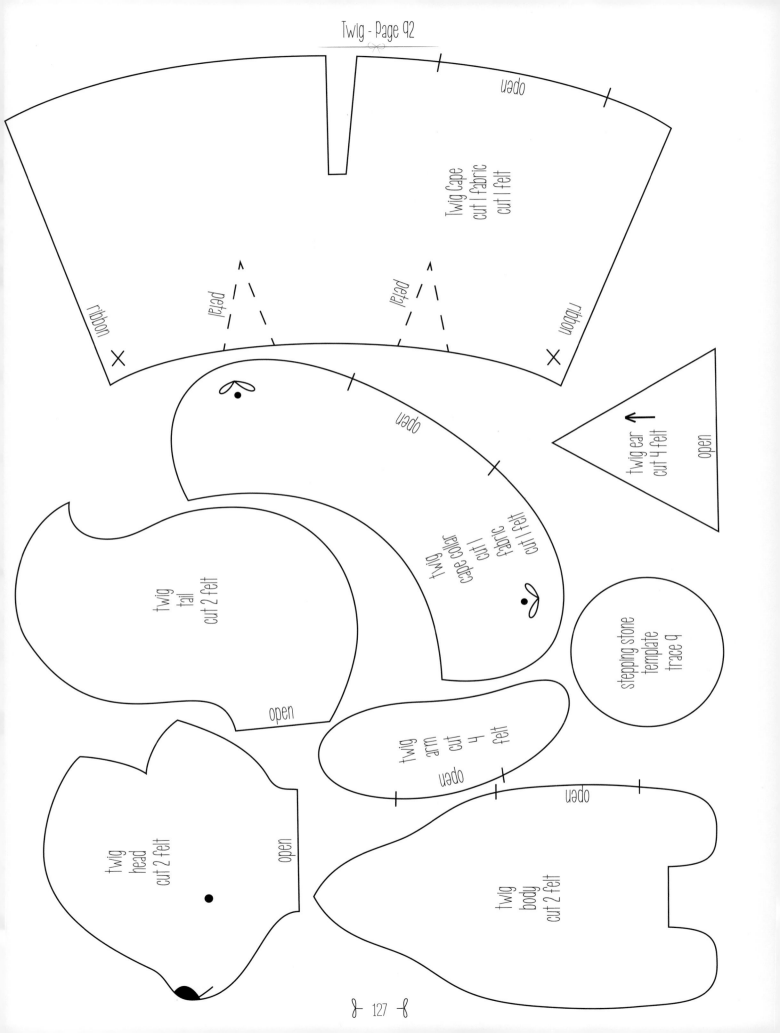

Twig Cape
cut 1 fabric
cut 1 felt

ribbon

petal

petal

ribbon

open

twig cape collar
cut 1 fabric
cut 1 felt

open

Twig ear
cut 4 felt

open

twig
tail
cut 2 felt

open

stepping stone
template
trace 9

twig
arm
cut 4
felt

open

twig
body
cut 2 felt

open

twig
head
cut 2 felt

open

suppliers

linen & fabric

The Cutting Cloth - www.thecuttingcloth.com.au

felt & and hedgehog fur

Winterwood - www.winterwoodtoys.com.au

pom poms

L'uccello - www.luccello.com.au

eyes

Bear Essence - www.bearessence.com.au

embroidery floss

Cosmo Embroidery Thread - www.etsy.com

vilene heavy backing & toy fill

Spotlight - www.spotlightstores.com

yarn

Jamieson's of Shetland - www.jamiesonsofshetland.co.uk

buttons

Vintage - www.etsy.com and my own collection